W. H. Anderdon

The seven ages of Clarewell

The history of a spot of ground

W. H. Anderdon

The seven ages of Clarewell
The history of a spot of ground

ISBN/EAN: 9783741178702

Manufactured in Europe, USA, Canada, Australia, Japa

Cover: Foto ©Lupo / pixelio.de

Manufactured and distributed by brebook publishing software
(www.brebook.com)

W. H. Anderdon

The seven ages of Clarewell

THE SEVEN AGES

OF

CLAREWELL;

THE

HISTORY OF A SPOT OF GROUND:

BY

REV. W. H. ANDERDON, M.A.

LONDON:

BURNS, OATES AND COMPANY,
17 PORTMAN STREET, AND 63 PATERNOSTER ROW.

1868.

ERRATA.

Page 13, line 12, *for* held *read* hold.
,, 63, ,, 9, *for* gives *read* give.
,, 121, ,, 21, *for* pleasunce *read* pleasaunce.
,, 124, ,, 6, *for* closed *read* cloud.
,, 135, ,, 6, *for* Innocent IV. *read* Innocent VI.

The Seven Ages of Clarewell.

AGE THE FIRST: 1236.

FORETOLD.

(*THE FOREST ROUND THE WELL*).

FIRST HUNTSMAN.

Wo-soa! wo-soa!—this way!

SECOND HUNTSMAN.

Nay, I saw his horns glance through the brake, down yonder. A stag of eight tine, I judge.

THIRD HUNTSMAN.

Wrong, both of you: hark to the old hound! there goes his deep mouth: never knew him out, yet. Away, there! sharp to the left!

PRICKER.

'Tis a cross scent he's come upon. But let us after. Aye, there go the rest, all together.

SECOND HUNTSMAN.

Follow, follow! Wo-soa, wo-soa!

HART (in the thicket).

Pant, pant, pant, pant, pant! pit-a-pat, pit-a-pat, pit-a-pat, pit-a-pat!

EARL HENRY.

Well leapt, my gallant bay! but we got among the bushes, down by that stream; we've been distanced, for once in our lives. Come, my lord, I promised you some English hunting, and you have hardly yet seen an English stag.

HART.

Pant, pant, pant, pant! pit-a-pat, pit-a-pat, pit-a-pat!

COUNT ROGER.

You have mounted me well, at least, noble Earl. Your island home, spite of the difficulties of transport, is stocked with a right excellent breed of horses. And need be, too, to follow such fleet stags as he that hath led us on to-day's chase. Eh, me! we must have run three full leagues without drawing bridle.

HART.

Pant, pant, pant! pit-a-pat, pit-a-pat!

EARL HENRY.

More than fourteen miles of English ground, believe me.

COUNT ROGER.

Did I not fear scorn from your stout huntsmen and foresters, if the French stranger seemed to give in—

EARL HENRY.

Concern not thyself at that, my noble friend. My vassals are used to see me dismount at any pause in the chase, and follow the fancy of the moment, while they wait around.

HART.

Pant, pant! pit-a-pat, pit-a-pat!

EARL HENRY.

At times, I throw myself on the green sward, under some spreading tree; and indulge a day-dream, if not wearied enough to sleep outright. Know you what such a day-dream means?

HART.

Pant, pant! pit-a-pat! I've almost got second wind now—I think I'll make a push for it. There come the hounds again; the right way this time. I'll make for the well, and the old man who lives by it!

Count Roger.

Aye, that do I. *Reveries*, we call them; it means the same. Not a minstrel, nor a troubadour, but hath his reverie. It takes him away from the present moment, from the turmoils of life, into a realm of fancy—

Hart.

Bounce, and away!

Earl Henry.

Halloo! halloo! there he goes, a gallant buck! ho, there!—where be those loitering knaves? All on the wrong scent! and my hounds? not fit to turn a spit at the kitchen fire!

Distant Horn.

Tra-ra-trill-a-la! trill-a-la!

Distant Huntsman.

Wo-soa! wo-soa! wo-soa!

Earl Henry.

Aye, blow and shout! yon stag hath gained a good mile of ground; he will be half way up Burnsleigh Hill, while ye toil on toward us.

Count Roger.

Be not vexed, my courteous host, with this mischance. The chase hath its haps and mishaps, even as more serious warfare: for my part, after our weary gallop, and on this calm evening—

CHAPEL BELL.

Tinkle-inkle-inkle:—tinkle-inkle-inkle:—tinkle-inkle-inkle!

COUNT ROGER.

In good time, comes the evening *Angelus.*

EARL HENRY.

The what? I knew not there was a chapel near.

COUNT ROGER.

Hush! down on our knees: *Angelus Domini nuntiavit Mariæ*—

CHAPEL BELL.

Tinkle-inkle-inkle:—tinkle-inkle-inkle:—tinkle-inkle-inkle!

COUNT ROGER.

Ecce ancilla Domini:—why answer ye not, my noble friend?

EARL HENRY.

I'm not over well versed in it—*Ave*—

HORN.

Tra-ra-trill-a-la! trill-a-la!

Chapel Bell.

Tinkle-inkle-inkle :— tinkle-inkle-inkle :— tinkle-inkle-inkle ! Tinkle ; tinkle ; tinkle !

Count Roger.

Yonder horn, that comes louder and louder, hath woefully broke in upon our evening prayer. But so it is: one moment, we are all for the next world ; the moment after, we return to be all for this. Well, then, which way?

Earl Henry.

I hardly know, more than yourself. This is a part of the forest the chase hath seldom led me into. I hear that an ancient holy man hath here established his cell; but never have I seen him. Let us seek the hermit now.

Count Roger.

With all my heart. The bell sounded from thereaway; if we can push through the tangled thicket—

Pricker.

My Lord, shall we couple up the hounds?

· Earl Henry

Do so, Wulfere; bid the hunt draw off, and bowne them homewards. Count Escremoville and

I will push towards yonder chapel. Bid our squires, and a couple more with arblasts, attend us.

Count Roger.

A thicket, indeed; and well named. Out, my good hunting sword, and lay about thee! One had need to ha' practised pioneering an army, to get through this tangle. See, my tunic of Lincoln green—call you it?—shows signs of having been in the wars.

Earl Henry.

Aye, these be not the open glades of Sherwood Forest, though they fringe it, where bold Robin Hood shot down many a royal buck, at the head of his merry men. That gentle outlaw, of whom my minstrel sang a "littel geste" to us, yester eve. At last, here we are, in a free space.

Count Roger.

How quiet a spot! It seems to have been cleared, as of trees, so of all obtrusive hindrances to meditation. Here might one dream life away; or, better still, pray it out to its end.

Earl Henry.

The spot is new to me.

Count Roger.

A little humble chapel, thatched with straw: a

young tree, lopped of its boughs, to form a rude cross:—ha! on that rough bench, the aged hermit, with a book older than himself.

EARL HENRY.

God give you good e'en, reverend father.

HERMIT.

And you, my sons, both. I have heard your horns waking up these woods the best part of an hour.

COUNT ROGER.

We, on our part, heard your *Angelus*, calling us from such vanities to prayer.

HERMIT.

Which you obeyed, to your souls' health?

EARL HENRY.

Hm,—as well as I knew how, at the moment. It was something new to me.

HERMIT.

What, praying my son?

EARL HENRY,

Not quite that: though I would I were more practised in it. But your particular *Angelus:* what means the bell?

Count Roger.

I take no credit for happening to have heard it before. You must know, I am a pilgrim lately come from Rome. A vow which I made during danger of shipwreck took me thither: and passing near, I turned aside to a town called Assisi—

Hermit.

Aye, Assisi?

Count Roger.

A place illustrious for the life and miracles of a great Saint, one Francis: so called from his proficiency in my native tongue. He passed from the earth some ten years agone; but not before he had established a multitude of houses of a new Order of brethren, of his own foundation. They live very poor and mortified, and—

Earl Henry.

So; methinks a wandering palmer told me somewhat of such men. Only, he laid the scene, not in Italy, but in your own scarce less sunny France, and called them the poor men of Lyons.

Hermit.

Nay, my son; there you are altogether astray. They of whom you now speak are but wolves in sheep's clothing: and by their pretended austerity draw the deluded ones who run after them, into manifest peril of heresy.

EARL HENRY.

Such things are beyond me. One poor man who chooses to be poor is very like another poor man who chooses it also.

HERMIT.

Hardly, son, if the Church sanctions the one for his obedience, and condemns the other for his contumacy. Does not that make all the difference?

COUNT ROGER.

Doubtless, father: my noble friend and I are both agreed. We be none of your Albigenses, nor poor men of Lyons, neither. For myself, I have thought more than once of taking the Cross against those misbelievers, and aiding to clear my native France of their pestilent foot-tracks.

HERMIT.

So far as they prove incapable of being reduced by milder measures. But I love better a gentle persuasion, and much prayer for them that are astray. A religious man, one Dominic, hath armed himself with the rosary, and gone forth to do spiritual battle against them.

COUNT ROGER.

But how if they yield not to such weapons? for it is the nature of heretics to be obstinate in the extreme.

HERMIT.

Nay, then, my son, I would say, God speed your arms.

EARL HENRY.

I, too, would cry "Saint George for merry England," as I spurred into any fair field. Yet, methinks, give me my choice, I had rather turn my sword against the false paynim who held captive the Sepulchre of the Lord; or the perfidious Jew, or any dog of Mahoud, wherever found—than hew down a baptised man because he held not with me in every particular.

COUNT ROGER.

Our late good king,* at least, seemed to think such an object worthy the sword of a Christian prince; for one of the latest actions of his life was to declare war against these misbelievers: which

---

* Louis VIII of France, who died a good and Christian death in 1226, leaving the succession to his young son, Louis IX, afterwards canonised at St. Louis. The regent here mentioned was Blanche of Castille.

the queen regent that now is, hath prosecuted with vigour in the name of her son.

Hermit.

And he, notwithstanding his youth, the troublous state of the kingdom, and his own peaceful disposition, is said already to turn his eyes to the East, and meditate an expedition to the Holy Land. So that in both directions, it will be his glory to unsheath the sword against the enemies of our holy religion.

Earl Henry.

How is it, now, reverend hermit, that you men of peace, the sanctity of whose cloth would be stained by so much as a drop of blood, are sometimes found to encourage the shedding of it, aye, in copious streams?

Hermit.

But when, my son?

Earl Henry.

Nay, let me see: why, again and again. Did not Saint Bernard preach the Crusade throughout France and Germany: and have not the Crusades spilled oceans of blood, and sent innumerable souls to the abyss?

Hermit.

When milder measures were powerless. It is the

glory, as well as duty, of Christian powers to protect their subjects from their deadliest enemies.

EARL HENRY.

Enemies?

HERMIT.

Aye, surely. What can be more fatal to a man than error in religion? That doth, indeed, plunge him down into the abyss. Who, then, is man's greater human enemy than the teacher of misbelief, who thrusts him thither? Who his greater human friend, than the lawful authority, that beareth not the sword in vain; but, even with its keen edge, assists in "rightly dividing the word of truth?"

EARL HENRY.

You seem to be quoting from some writer. I read, not I; nay, not a letter: yet would I fain know who hath penned the words.

HERMIT.

One whose pen was guided by the Holy Ghost: the apostle Paul. I noted the words, some years since, from a fair manuscript in the scriptorium of that very Assisi, where *you*, my son, paid your devotions.

COUNT ROGER.

You, too, have been in that holy spot?

HERMIT.

I made some months of novitiate there, till it was manifested to me that my path was to be a solitary one. I left it, with much sorrow; and pushed hitherward, intending a voyage to Ireland, to spend my days on that lake* where, they say, the unseen world makes itself visible to those who seek it by fast and prayer.

COUNT ROGER.

So found yourself here, to our advantage, who crave your blessing on this calm evening.

EARL HENRY.

Do you not sometimes wish for the companionship of those you left behind?

HERMIT.

My son, when a man has once ascertained what the Dispenser of callings would have him do, let him not consult with flesh and blood: nor ask himself on what paths his own tastes would lead him. We all have our vocation. Mine is to serve God here, and alone. "No man, having put his

---

Lough Dearg, with its island, containing "Saint Patrick's purgatory," for centuries a favourite place of pilgrimage and penitential exercises.

hand to the plough, and looking back, is fit for the kingdom of God."

COUNT ROGER.

Methinks, it must be a hard matter for a man to tell what may be his vocation in life.

HERMIT.

For a man to tell: but not so hard for another man to tell him.

EARL HENRY.

Another man?

HERMIT.

Aye, his confessarius, of course: who, if he exercise his ministry with prayer, will not fail to discover in which direction the Lord is leading the soul He hath entrusted to him. But there is something in your eye, my son, that goes beyond the words of your question.

COUNT ROGER.

Nay, as you scan me thus narrowly, I hold it no shame to own, in the presence of my courteous friend, such a doubt often perplexeth me as to myself.

EARL HENRY.

How, then; is not your state of life yet fixed?

Count Roger.

A bow-shot from my ancestral castle in Lorraine rise the humble walls of a house of those same cordeliers of Saint Francis. Such instruction as I have received, I owe to those mortified men. Whatever good has kept me from more evil than swells my account, is through them. To their charity I have confided the troubles of my conscience, and the fluctuations of my heart. And their hands have girt me, all sinful layman though I be, with the cord and scapular of their Third Order—

Earl Henry.

And you have taken their vows? Your eye is too bright, and your bugle rings too cheerily thro' the green wood, to let me think it.

Hermit.

So do they deem, who will have it that to serve the Lord of all loveliness and joy, to love Him and be loved by Him, must needs be a thing of gloom. Art thou of that number?

Count Roger.

Nay, my reverend father: the noble Earl doth himself scant justice: for—

Hermit.

I believe it well. Report gives out Earl Henry

as a man not indevout, nor rebellious against his spiritual mother, the Church.

EARL HENRY.

Albeit, my censors might add, I go not so far as our good king* in his unlimited deference to Rome; and hold half a score of bishops a match for one legate—

HERMIT.

Nay, it is not for me to add anything, my son. If I find, not uncommonly, in England, a certain proud and insular independence, which trenches even too near the sacred deposit of the faith—

COUNT ROGER.

Permit me to claim the privilege of a foreigner and a guest, and save my noble friend from a public confession. Moreover, if there be in this land any lack of filial devotion to the Holy See, then, as a Frenchman, I accept a full share of the blame. I fear me, the coming of my Norman fellow-country-

---

* Henry III, of whom Matthew Paris, (an untrustworthy writer in this particular, says Dod. *History*, I, 120) tells us that his devotion to the legate, Otho, as representing the Holy See, caused much uneasiness, and at length open clamours, among his subjects. These were quieted by a letter from the king to Innocent IV, for the adjustment of certain canonical points in question.

men hath not improved the religion of the island. The Saxon Church was more filial, and fruitful.

Hermit.

My children, let us see things clearly. A legate comes into the kingdom, as into any other Christian realm, to represent the father of all, and visible head of all. No provincial bishops, nay, be they in synod assembled—can lawfully oppose the will of the Supreme Pontiff, thus made known to them. The fault of our good king (if indeed it beseem his subjects to sift them) is, not that he yields unlimited deference to a voice from Rome, but that he remains at the mercy of lay favourites, and chiefly foreigners. Three years ago, the Poitevin nobles, following the steps of their countryman Des Roches, set the kingdom in a blaze of jealous indignation. Still later, our king's marriage with Eleanor of Provence hath filled the court, so I am told, and the offices of state, with her Provençal followers. I fear not to speak thus in presence of my French guest; for he knows well, an old man in a hermitage belongs rather to the universal family than to any nation.

Count Roger.

Add, that the cord of Francis is the further bond between us. Moreover, my noble friend and I have striven to emulate the hault friendship of our several monarchs, who, even when at war with one another, have never broken the link of mutual Christian charity.

EARL HENRY.

My king hath always found in Louis his dearest friend and lay adviser, in all that concerned not the actual debate between their crowns.

COUNT ROGER.

And I, in turn, confess that at a late conference between them, when their words turned upon spiritual things, King Henry had the manifest advantage.

HERMIT.

Of what speak you, my son?

COUNT ROGER.

It is said, the English king hears three Masses daily, beside his other acts of devotion and charity. At the time I speak of, my king asked his brother of England, why he preferred to hear so many masses rather than at least one sermon? Because, quoth King Henry, I had rather converse with my Friend face to face, than hear about Him through the lips of another.

HERMIT.

A noble and pious saying. Would he might be inspired at mass to give more ear to the holy Edmund, Archbishop of Canterbury,* whom our Holy Father, now happily reigning, hath moved to plead with him on behalf of his subjects' rights!

EARL HENRY.

Strange, that with so much piety there should be so little strength.

HERMIT.

Your knight's chain, my son, is of pure gold, I doubt not; though here and there a link be feeble.

COUNT ROGER.

A monarch that is strong, yet Christian, is *rara avis in terris*.

HERMIT.

Personal strength, and force of will, are perilous weapons, even as a two-edged sword. Safe are we, while we feel our weakness, and are kept lowly thereby.

---

* Edmund Rich, who died in exile at Soissy, and was buried at Pontigny in 1242, having vainly endeavoured, at the instance of Pope Gregory IX, to plead with the king for the liberties of the country against the undue foreign influence that was oppressing it. He was canonised by Innocent V, four years after his death.

EARL HENRY.

Meanwhile, father, will you not exercise the virtue of hospitality, and permit us to taste your hermit-fare?

HERMIT.

It should have been thought on before, my children. Come into my poor hut, with an old man's welcome; though the fare, as well as lodging, be of the poorest—ha! beware the lintel!

EARL HENRY.

Nay, it hath but struck my hunting-cap from the head that should have stooped lower: a fit commentary on your words, and thus I accept it. We hold our heads too high, Count, in this world. But what do I see? the very hart we have chased so long to-day, now lying at his ease in the corner! Pardon, reverend father: we knew not we were following your tame favourite.

HERMIT.

All God's dumb creatures are favoured here, with small distinction. This poor beast, hard pressed, hath fled hither, almost for the first time. The altar is an asylum, even for malefactors, till the first heat of the avenger be overpast: how much more for the guiltless? For what saith the psalm?

"The sparrow hath found herself an house;
And the turtle a nest for herself, where she may lay her young:
Thy altars, O Lord of hosts, my King and my God."

COUNT ROGER.

Besides being holy writ, that is also Franciscan observance. How gentle was our seraphic Father to all living things! how would they come from the forest and the air, and crowd around him! the timid fawn gazing up into his eyes, the shy dove pluming its wing on his shoulder, the chattering sparrow nestling within the folds of his coarse grey frock—

HERMIT.

Macte virtute, my son: thou speakest like a true brother of the cord. And, doubtless, in proportion as man is cleansed from offence against the Maker of all life, he reconciles to himself again the creatures who fled from him in Paradise, when he had lost his title to life here and hereafter.

EARL HENRY.

Truly, as I listen, I could well nigh be weaned from hunting, as mere savagery, and mimic war.

Count Roger.

Fear not, brother: many a cheer will we yet give to the hounds in their full music; many a stirring blast yet wind on the horn, if all goes well!

Hermit.

Meanwhile, what tidings from beyond seas?

Count Roger.

Nothing so peaceful as sparrows nestling and chattering under church-eaves, or in Franciscan habits. What think you of a bloody fray among the students in Paris, cordeliers, as well as others, in which many heads have been broken, and some lives lost—all about the writings of a Greek sage, whose name escapes me?

Hermit.

Aye, he of Stagyra, whose great mind hath formed the system of the schools. But can they, indeed, have proceeded to such extremes in that University? I remember it in more peaceful days, when the great Alexander Hales, "Irrefragable Doctor," sat so worthily in the chair of canon law: and was as little to be overcome in logic as his royal namesake in war.

COUNT ROGER.

Nay, the actual violence I speak of was a few years past: but the heat continues.

HERMIT.

Thus doth man think to promote a search after truth, by breaking the first of the commandments regarding his neighbour: as if the wrath of man could work the righteousness of God!

EARL HENRY.

Except against Turks and Albigenses.

HERMIT.

My master, Alexander? Is he still in life?

COUNT ROGER.

Not only so, but in that of religion.

HERMIT.

How? in religion?

COUNT ROGER.

I marvel, no tidings of it have reached thee. Some fifteen years back, he took the habit of Assisi: and now he teaches at Paris in the grey frock, with no less fame and concourse of disciples than you describe of his early days.

Earl Henry.

So, it appeareth the grey frock is to prevail over the knightly baldric, and the ermine of nobles! Up, then, Count! let us fulfil our destiny. Take we, if not the cross against the unbeliever, yet—

Count Roger.

The scapular against that slothful and lukewarm *Self*, who is Christendom's worst enemy.

Hermit.

Many a true word is spoken in jest, son of mine.

Earl Henry.

The sooner the better;

"Car tous les vaillants sont en voyage:"

and meanwhile, the sun is declining, and warns us to be away.

Count Roger.

With your leave, reverend father, I will not quit Earl Henry's castle without seeking your cell again.

Hermit.

Welcome always, my son.

Earl Henry.

Have you no request to proffer to me on parting? My woodsmen and rangers shall come and build up your cell stronger, against the inclement season: the master-mason, who now buildeth a turret to my castle, shall enlarge the bason of the well whence you have given us so pure a draught.

Hermit.

Earl Henry! man builds and plants, as though he were lord of the earth whereon he creeps; and lo! by next spring he hath gone under that very earth, and the trees have budded round his tomb.

Earl Henry.

A prophecy, father, or a sermon?

Count Roger.

The Cross be between us and harm!

Hermit.

Aye, its power be on us, to mortify ambition and the pride of life. Build churches, my son, for your vassals; let your woodmen repair the tenements of such as be poor against their will. For me, I lack nothing: and so, *Benedicite.*

EARL HENRY.

..Yet permit me to do somewhat for you, if only to repair for my too froward speech!

HERMIT.

One thing, and that alone. When, some day, I shall be found dead by the chance wayfarer, send your masons to protect with stone-work this well, of which I have drunk my daily draught in my solitude.

EARL HENRY.

It shall be done, father hermit, for your sake.

HERMIT.

Not for mine: but for those who shall come after. Mark me, Earl. The heart that converses not with its kind gains somewhat of forecasting for its silence and loneliness. In my dreams, in my prayers, I seem to see this spot inhabited by Franciscan brothers, who shall sing the praises of God day and night, when I am laid to sleep in the earth beside this well.

EARL HENRY.

Fancies, perchance; perchance realities. Some descendant of my own may be the founder.

Hermit.

He will be blessed in the deed. Give thou this land to God, and this well. I have dedicated it to a holy virgin yet living in Assisi, named Clare; who, if I mistake not, will die in the odour of sanctity. Let the place be named, Clarewell. There shall one day arise here a cloister of Friars Minor, not unworthy their name and cord.

Earl Henry.

Clarewell it shall be. My chaplain shall draw the deed of gift: and albeit the wars have so impoverished me, that I may not hope to see the foundation-stone, yet shall it be laid up in the time to come.

Count Roger.

Amen. I am joyful witness of this gift to God.

Hermit.

One day is with the Lord as a thousand years, and a thousand years as one day.

Earl Henry.

So let us to horse, and away. A stirrup-cup from Clare's Well!

Hermit.

With an old man's benison.

The Seven Ages of Clarewell.

AGE THE SECOND: 1336.

BUILT.

(SOUTH-WEST GARDEN WALL, NEAR THE POSTERN LEADING FROM CLOISTER INTO GARDEN.)

LAY-BROTHER.

So! a pretty load, and from a good distance. I never reckoned it so far to the outer gate before.

UNDER-MASON.

I thought this was silence-time. May one talk?

LAY-BROTHER.

Oh, yes: until the first bell. Then I go in; and I assure you, I shall be fain to hear it toll for meditation. These be weighty stones!

UNDER-MASON.

And of a good grain, if laid as they lay in the

quarry. All depends, look you, on the lie of the grain.

LAY-BROTHER.

Help me, now, with this big one, here. Together—heave, ho!

UNDER-MASON.

You seem to find it enough to do. Why, I understood you had a hardish life before coming here. My trowel, please.

LAY-BROTHER.

Hard life? yes, but then—

UNDER-MASON.

Tick, tick, tick! Now, I think this one lies pretty square. Would you hand the plumb-line this way?

BEE.

Z-z o-o o-o m-m! not much to be found here: seems a new place altogether. Nothing but chips and shavings all about. Z-z o-o o-o m-m!

LAY-BROTHER.

One gets older and stiffer, as time flies. Now—

BEE.

Z-z o-o o-o m-m! not a sprig of rosemary, nor a wall-flower! well, better luck next spring! Z-z o-o m-m!

Lay-Brother.

That barrow of stones wouldn't have cost me even a long breath to wheel it the same distance, five years agone.

Under-Mason.

Five years of fasting, tick, tick, tick-a-tick! with all the rest of it tick! tick! must make inroads, even on a strong man, methinks. A Lent, all the year round, would soon do for me. Now then, for this other large one: heave-ho!

Swallow.

Snap! aha, master May-fly! I thought I shouldn't miss you twice running!

Lay-Brother.

Oh, it isn't that: you would not feel the observances of our life, when once in the regular train of them. Besides, the absence of all care. The bell rings you up, rings you about, rings you through the day, rings you to bed again—

Under-Mason.

Heave-oh! there:—so the day must be like my neighbour Hodge's mill-wheel, round and round:— plumb-line, please: aye, that one lies square enough —or, like the old mill-horse, tick, tick-a-tick! that is put into the collar, to do the work, tick-a-tick! when the mill-stream is dry.

BEE.

Z-z o-o o-o o-o m-m!

UNDER-MASON.

Doth it grow wearisome, now, in the long run—one day so like another?

MASON.

Chip, chip-a-chip! a tidyish oak-leaf, this, chip-a-chip! though I say it that shouldn't. It will be many a long year before the young saplings the somptner has planted at the grange below will bear—chip-a-chip!—such a full good leaf. And mine don't wither, nor fall in the autumn, eh?—chip-a-chip! I shall leave my mason's mark here, just under it, for future times to wonder at:—chip-a-chip! there!

Sing hey, sing ho! for the the merry green woo-oods
Chip-a-chip! chip-a-chip!
of Stafford-shee-ee-re! chip-a-chip!

SUB-WARDEN.

You need not take half so much trouble about that window-head, my good friend. I hardly like so much ornament on it: it is only to be the window of the store-room. Not another stroke.

MASON.

Not finish this oak-leaf, father? why, it's all in the rough. I am working by the piece, and for the love of the thing. So the ornament is nothing out of the coffers of Saint Francis.

SUB-WARDEN.

No, my son; thanks—I know it. That is what makes it easier for me to speak. You wish to please Saint Francis: so do I. We must try to please him, each in our own way. You bring your chisel and your taste, your skill and zeal, and devote them to the wants of his spiritual children—

SWALLOW.

Snap! not so bad: a fine blue-bottle.

SUB-WARDEN.

Meanwhile, I must take care to secure what our seraphic Father loves better than anything material: that spirit of entire poverty, and contempt of the false goods of earth, which he left us for our precious inheritance.

MASON.

Now, I should think it poverty enough to possess nothing of my own, not so much as the latchet of a sandal—aye, even if the convent building I shared with others were carved in stone fret-work from end to end.

Sub-Warden.

So did not our sainted founder. He knew how insensibly, and in what subtle wise, *Self* creeps in at every chink, unless we be on the watch to turn it out. Out we have it at door; in it flies at window. Out we fling it at window; in it creeps by the key-hole. In it can creep by art, even religious art; and by architecture, even Church architecture—

Swallow.

Snap! snap! well done; right and left. That's almost enough, till supper.

Sub-Warden.

And by beauty, even spiritual and consecrated beauty.

Under-Mason.

Heave, ho! I wish they could invent something better than poor mason's thews and sinews to heave stones into their places. That powder, now, that a monk in Germany (they told me when I worked at Cologne) found the way to make, some five years ago, as he was compounding sulphur and things in a mortar. Why, he nearly blew off his own head by mistake, and lifted the roof of his convent. That sort of stuff might heave up stones rarely, methinks,—if you could only get it well under.

Lay-Brother.

Powder? why, our Roger Bacon, the great friar for all sorts of marvels, wrote about that kind of thing, nigh an hundred years ago, they say: and about carriages that could be made to go without horses, and no one knows what besides. For my part, I can't believe a tithe of what he wrote.

Under-Mason.

You read, then, like the fathers?

Lay-Brother.

Not I; but I listen to what is read in the refectory: one picks up a surprising deal, by that means, in the course of six months.

Sub-Warden.

By your face, my good Richard, I see, 'tis a hard bit of doctrine I've been giving you.

Mason.

Well, father—if every one thought like you—

Sub-Warden.

It would put an end to the noble handicraft?

LAY-BROTHER.

Don't whisper, even. I want to hear. Plumb-line, a moment.

UNDER-MASON.

Answer me, quite low. Why won't he let him finish carving that window-head?

LAY-BROTHER.

'Gainst poverty—hush!

MASON.

How can I make answer to a reverend and learned divine? but when I wrought for the Cistercians at Bolton, and the Benedictine chapter at—

SUB-WARDEN.

Nay, I judge not my neighbour; nor would I criticise the spirit of other Orders in the Church. "Let every spirit praise the Lord." I speak as a poor brother of Saint Francis, and about the window of our store-room.

UNDER-MASON.

Quiet, now: plumb-line.

SUB-WARDEN.

Hear the words of our Rule: "All the brothers are to be clad in mean habits, and may blessedly mend them with sacks, and other pieces: whom I admonish and exhort, that they do not despise nor censure such men as they see clad in curious and gay garments, and using delicate meats and drinks, but rather let every one judge and despise himself." Seest thou why we censure not carved stone-work, though we carve it not?

MASON.

There be Whitby, now, and Tynemouth—

SUB-WARDEN.

Whitby was founded by Saint Hilda herself: be it richly adorned, that men may honour by stone-work one whom God hath so enriched by His grace.

MASON.

And Tynemouth?

SUB-WARDEN.

They have digged, I am told, great store of coal out of the lands of our Benedictine brethren at Newcastle, to which that place is an haven.* Coal

* Mention is made in 1325, of the exportation of coal from Newcastle to France: the first leases of coal works in that neighbourhood are dated a few years later. They were granted by the monks of Tynemouth to various persons at annual rents, ranging from two to about five pounds. In 1327, ten shilings' worth of Newcastle coal was purchased for the coronation of Edward III.

is of the nature of *treasure trove:* the earth itself hath yielded them the means to raise great monuments to God's glory above its surface. In brief, they of Tynemouth follow their Rule and spirit, as we try to follow ours: for all which things the Lord be praised.

Second Bee.

Z-z o-o o-o m-m! my sister was quite right—nothing to be got—that warm corner, though, would be a pleasant place, if we swarmed from our community next year—make a note of it—z-z o-o m-m!

Sub-Warden.

Poverty is the meat and drink, as silence is the very atmosphere and breath, of every Order and community that means to survive—

Under-Mason.

As quiet as we can—tick, tick-a-tick! one musn't stand idle, though, but I dearly want to listen.

Sub-Warden.

We are just founding ourselves here; and by the blessing of heaven, we mean to survive.

Under-Mason.

Tick, tick! tick-a-tick!

Sub-Warden.

They would be fatal enemies, in the guise of friends, who should lure us, by gifts, or any temporal aid, from the Lady Poverty whom Saint Francis wooed so enthusiastically, his life long. From poor Grey friars we should grow into cultivated men of art; and then—

Under-Mason.

Whoop! how near that marten flew! I could have nicked him with my trowel.

Marten.

That's a snug corner the fellow is building: I'll come back next spring, for another look. If they run it up a second story, it will be high and safe enough for a nest—

Mason.

And then—you say, father, what would happen then?

Marten.

The aspect, I should judge, W.S.W. or thereabouts: and would suit me better than the battlements of Windsor Castle, where the men-at-arms are always practising at us with their cross-bows.

Lay-Brother.

How the creature screams and whirls round the

cloister! Saint Francis would bid it be silent, and let us hear what the Sub-Warden is saying.

Sub-Warden.

Then? why, I am no prophet: but I can read something of the future by the past: and any one can interpret the fate and fortunes of our Order by the known will and spirit of its sainted founder.

Marten.

Off, now! to Scotland, of which these earth-plodders know nothing.

Sub-Warden.

Such reflected light is enough for me to walk by. As to things in general, it is out of my way to speculate on them.

Warden.

Things in general, Father Sub-Warden, by which I take you to mean *principles*, would help us a good way to the solution.

Both Masons.

Your blessing, reverend Father: and on our homes and families.

Sub-Warden.

We did not hear you come down the walk,

Father Warden. You come in time to settle, not an abstract question, but a practical point, on which I should have sought your paternity in another moment: the amount of carving to be expended on this window.

Warden.

Let us reach the conclusion through the avenue down which I was mentally pacing when I came upon you so noiselessly.

Lay-Brother.

Now, a whisper in your ear. He'll no more let Richard Mason go on with his carving than the Sub-Warden; nay, of the two, somewhat less.

Under-Mason.

Like enough: methinks, I see it in his eye.

Third Bee.

Z-z o-o m-m! I'm told, there's nothing to be got here—thought I'd just top the wall, and try. No flowers—but dear me! out of that window comes a smell of last year's apples. I'll nip in, and look about me—z-z o-o o-o m-m!

Under-Warden.

Have at you, there! no? ah-f! that gritty stone!

SUB-WARDEN.

Cruel fellow! I am heartily glad you missed it: I can scarce be sorry you hit your hand such a thwack against the mullion.

BEE.

Z-z-z! you will, will you? take that, then! z-z-z!

UNDER-MASON.

Hey! hey! o-oh! ha, I got you, at last, you varmint!

DYING BEE.

Zwz-wz-wz-wz-wz-wz!

SUB-WARDEN.

What right have you to take away the life of one of God's creatures, that did not harm you first, nor could be of any use to you?

UNDER-MASON.

'Tis a shrewd smart, though—hey!

SUB-WARDEN.

And what a thing is man, that destroys all beneath him, stings all that are round him—

WARDEN.

And neglects and forgets all that is above him.

Well, brother Felix, take this good fellow, who has learned mercy to the next bee he meets; take him to Saint Clare's Well, and dip his hand. It has performed more difficult cures, before now.

Lay-Brother.

Truly, father. There was the miller's son, that had the falling sickness; and the poor little child that was brought all the way from Carlisle—

Warden.

My son Richard, you seem in a brown study.

Mason.

Reverend lord—

Warden.

Nay, not that: only a poor brother of Saint Francis. But what is it?

Sub-Warden.

He is thinking about our discouraging his art. You promised us a walk down your avenue of thought, Father Warden. I fancy, as we go along, we shall clear up *his* thoughts for him.

Fourth Bee.

Z-z o-o m-m! Smell of fruit! apples and pears! in through this window! z-z o-o m-m!

SUB-WARDEN.

Courage, friend Richard! Did we not let you have your own way (pretty much) in our new church? did you not carve angels in the choir, and vices and demons in the gurgoyles, to your heart's content? Why, half the children in the hamlet were afraid, for some time, to go in at the west door, all because of the great dragon that you made to gnash and writhe so under the spear of Saint Michael!

MASON.

I should enjoy a walk with Father Warden, whatever point it led to.

WARDEN.

We can walk through a whole avenue, while we are quietly seated. Here, let us seat ourselves on this beam, which is one day to support the refectory roof:—under the very window in question. Ready? let us set out.

MASON.

My oak-leaf has a bad chance, I fear.

WARDEN.

Step the first; "Every kingdom divided against itself, is brought to desolation: and house upon house shall fall." Eh?

AGE THE SECOND—BUILT.

MASON.

That's good masonry, so far as I understand it.

WARDEN.

Step the second; Therefore every association, state or community, that is not an unhealthy growth of time, like a wart on a tree, nor thrown together like drift-wood and weeds on a sea-beach, proceeds—

FIRST SPARROW.

Chirrup! how earnestly those three are laying their heads together! I wish the old shaven man would move a little further from that open window: one might have a chance of getting in. Didn't you see that bee go in just now?

SECOND SPARROW.

Chirrup, chirrup!

WARDEN.

Proceeds on some first principle, or ruling idea, as the condition of its life and permanence.

Step the third: this primary idea, if sound, and based on reason and truth, secures to the aggregation of men who shall be gathered round it, or moulded upon it, a fair chance of continuing.

Step the fourth: over and above mere continuance, which is (so far) secured by its reasonableness, the degree to which it promises good results, to those engaged in such a community life, and to others beyond them, is in proportion to the vitality of that first principle.

Bee, coming out again.

Z-z o-o o-o m-m!

Second Sparrow.

Chirrup! here's a chance for me: no!—he's dodged back. Wait a bit! chirrup!

Warden.

Step the fifth: The better thing than reasonableness, which promises higher results, and without which nothing succeeds, in our sense of *success*, is *Faith*. Christian faith, which leads to Christian charity, and Christian mortification.

Bee, out through the window.

Z-z o-o m-m! now home, and tell her majesty what a store I've found—z-z o-o—

First Sparrow.

Chirrup! not so fast! Fresh bee, with apple-sauce—no bad luncheon!

Warden.

Step the sixth: Now, among religious orders, each

with its distinctive character, though all with so much in common, we children of Saint Francis are to be noted for the spirit of poverty. We may be learned or ignorant: that is accidental, in a sense—

MASON.

Truly, reverend father, it is only yourself, in your humility, who could say it. Wherever I go, I hear of the frock of Saint Francis teaching in the schools, with concourse of disciples round their chairs. At Oxenforde, they tell me, the Friars Minor have, for one hundred years, and more—

WARDEN.

By the mercy of God, we have had our share in the instruction of youth. But it enters not into our first idea: it lay not so near the heart of our Seraphic father as the poverty for which he left all this earth affords. The family of the great Saint Benedict is vowed to poverty, even as to their other religious vows, in their degree, of course; for they are monks—

MASON.

I would I might chip and carve for you as for them!

WARDEN.

They also cultivate learning, and have thus been

the preservers of many precious remains of antiquity, when barbarism over-ran the old Roman Empire:—

MASON.

Aye, I have had a touch at their library windows, before now: *they* are not afraid of knops, now, and roses, on the mullions!

WARDEN.

Our dear brothers, the sons of Saint Dominic, are specially styled the Friars Preachers; like their holy and zealous founder, they have gone forth against heresy with "the sword of the Spirit, which is the word of God." But we—

MASON.

You make me a spoiled child, Father, by the kindness of your speech; I venture to break in upon your words again. Where do we find greater preachers than among the Friars Minor? Their burning words, in their own churches, and through the land, do they not draw crowds to listen, and then to seek them in holy confession? Was there not, for one ensample only, brother William Gainsborough, sent for to Rome, before he was anointed Bishop of Worcester, forasmuch as his learning and eloquence—

WARDEN.

Hey, my son? and how hast thou become thyself so learned and eloquent on this topic?

MASON.

Nay, father, they be but scraps I have picked up here and there, amid my work. But he must be purblind, as though a stone chip had flown into his eyes, who can go through England on building errands, and not mark how the Grey friars preach, teach in our universities, and draw men's souls after them.

WARDEN.

Shall I tell thee how? Nay, Saint Paul shall tell. "My speech, and my preaching, was not in the persuasive words of human wisdom, but in the showing of the Spirit and power: that your faith might not stand on the wisdom of men, but on the power of God. Howbeit, we speak wisdom among the perfect: yet not the wisdom of this world." That appears to me to be a portrait of the true Friar Minor.

MASON.

He contrives to persuade, though, and that mightily, in that same unpersuading way.

WARDEN.

His name implies that he is among the little ones

of earth. Now, on earth, nothing is less esteemed, nor more despised, than humility and poverty. *Ergo*, the Friar Minor is, above all things, to be lowly and poor. I think they would pick no hole in that syllogism, even at Oxenforde. Your finest chisel, my son, could not find a crack in it.

MASON.

Hm! I fain would try. Methinks, I know a monk in Oriel College, now newly built, who would dispute it with great show of *argumentorum*.

WARDEN.

So I come (nay, 'tis thou leadest me) to my seventh and last step; thus:

It is by following out this spirit of our Order in its strictness, that we both "save ourselves, and them that hear us." Thus have we gathered into our communities the choicest souls from other states of life, lay and ecclesiastical: who have come to us to learn the words: "Blessed be ye poor, for yours is the kingdom of heaven." You have mentioned some of them: what shall I say of others?

MASON.

Nay, I well believe, and partly know it.

WARDEN.

At the first foundation of our Order, in Italy, the

great, the learned, and the gay, came to us in crowds to woo Poverty, after our Father's ensample. So have they continued still to do. Ermine, and minever, and samite, gaudy trappings, knightly array, have all been doffed for the coarse habit and cord of the Grey Friar. Here in England, they would fill a list, could I stay to make it out.

MASON.

My grandfather lived at Canterbury when the Grey friars first landed, and settled themselves in the island of Bennewith. He hath told me things all out of the ordinary way, respecting their holy lives, and the esteem of them both by nobles and the common sort.

WARDEN.

A miracle converted an abbot of Abingdon* to resign his office, and exchange the habit of Saint Benedict for that of the mendicant friar. He passed from the Grey friars to the Church Triumphant—I trust—more than an hundred years agone; the very year when our great brother, Roger Bacon, joined us.† The next year came to us the Superior of the Canons Regular at Osney: nearer

---

* Robert de Hendred. His remarkable vocation is detailed in "Saint Francis and the Franciscans," pp. 248-9.

† A. D. 1234.

to our own day, Ralph Maydstone, Bishop of Hereford. So I might go on: but time would fail.

Mason.

Father, may I say a word?

Warden.

So many as it pleases you, until the bell rings for meditation, which methinks will be soon.

Mason.

'Twas but of late, then, a brother of my guild was at work at the Grey friars in Cornhill, within the City of London. You know, reverend father, better than I, how large a building, in room of the first and antient house, is being raised there, and now nigh finished, by the benefaction of Dame Margaret, widow of our King that was, the first Edward. She hath bequeathed to it one hundred marks, beside her former donations. And with this, aided by the piety of Dame Philippa, the Queen that now is, the Earl of Richmond, the Countess of Pembroke, the Lady Margaret Segrave—

Warden.

So good; so good:—may their benefactions be repaid to them an hundred-fold—as surely they will. But come on with thy conclusion.

Mason.

The Grey friars, then, in London, have built them an house—

Warden.

With ornaments in the window-head of the store-room? Nay, then, let them look to it, lest one day the greediness of this earth's proud ones—

Great Bell.

Toll !—toll !—toll !—toll !—toll !

Warden.

Hush ! *Benedicite*

The Seven Ages of Clarewell.

AGE THE THIRD: 1436.

OCCUPIED.

(THE GARDEN, SURROUNDED BY ITS ALLEY AND WALL).

Master of Novices.

The Presence of God! so let us always begin our recreation, in spirit as in words. What a fine spring afternoon!

First Novice.

And how full the place is of bees! why, the air seems alive as well as musical with them.

Second Novice.

Now, brother Antony, don't quote Virgil, if you can possibly help it: though the temptation *is* great.

ANTONY.

So great, that it consists of a whole Georgic, from the illuminated capital to the final flourish.

THIRD NOVICE.

Aye, such a flourish as you executed in the Scriptorium yesterday; endless whirligigs of red and blue, and a dragon devouring its own tail.

FOURTH NOVICE.

And a small ape between two particularly large strawberries.

FIFTH NOVICE.

Besides, we are never to quote at recreation. Why is that, by the way?

ANTONY.

Ask the Father. Father, brother Didacus has a question.

MASTER OF NOVICES.

Well?—well, my son, let us hear it?

DIDACUS.

Hardly fair, Antony: I asked *you*.

ANTONY.

And, of course, I passed the question on to the Father.

DIDACUS.

That's not what I call fair. Agnellus, will *you* tell me?

MASTER OF NOVICES.

You have to learn one or two things, dear Didacus, besides this particular question, whatever it be. A novice asks questions of his master, when they are worth asking at all. And now, looking at you, I seem to read your thoughts. Shall I interpret them for you?

DIDACUS.

Oh, father! I was wrong. I dare say you *did* read me, only too well.

MASTER OF NOVICES.

You thought within yourself: Why is a young man, because he is training to be a Friar Minor, to be thus perpetually under discipline—

DIDACUS.

Father!

MASTER OF NOVICES.

Headed back, and snubbed, at every turn—

DIDACUS.

Oh, father!

MASTER OF NOVICES.

Especially when, like me, his antecedents in the world have fitted him—

DIDACUS.

Please, father! oh, my unhappy tongue!

MASTER OF NOVICES.

One who has fought at Orleans, and Compiegne, and Caen, and Lagni; and so much distinguished himself that—

ANTONY.

Father, father! may I plead for him? I ought to have passed the question by.

MASTER OF NOVICES.

Well, my children, I spare you both. "A word is enough to the wise:" and you are learners in one of the highest branches of wisdom—the knowledge of yourselves.

AGNELLUS.

E cœlo descendit γνῶθι σεαυτόν.

MASTER OF NOVICES.

Is that no quotation? Come, it is time to walk, that we may free ourselves from some of this superfluous learning. Besides, the Warden and the professed are coming round this way. As we go down the walk, I will answer your question, and tell you why we don't quote at recreation.

Didacus.

Dear father, I—for one—am quite satisfied.

Antony, Agnellus, and the rest.

Oh, yes—all.

Master of Novices.

Not so. After an act of implicit submission, comes the reward of knowledge. Had our first parents taken that way of gaining it, we should have been in Paradise, not at Clarewell. But they had a little of the spirit of Didacus—

Didacus.

Or Didacus too much of the old Adam—

Master of Novices.

So, grasped at the shadow, and lost the substance. Now, as we walk down this path, listen. After your noviceship will come a distinct period of study, when the intellect, disciplined and prepared for the reception of truth by your present exercises in docility,—

WARDEN.

There they go, those good and dear youths: it makes my heart glad to follow them with my old eyes, that little flock. When we are laid in the cloister,—I, at least,—may they glorify God and Saint Francis here!

SUB-WARDEN.

They could hardly be in better hands than with brother Louis.

WARDEN.

He has, indeed, the authority of a father with the heart of a mother: they seem to thrive under such a tempered treatment of strictness and gentle love.

SUB-WARDEN.

Very different in their natural characters; yet all seem happy, and all are observant.

WARDEN.

May the novices of Clarewell be of the same spirit, even to the end!

SUB-WARDEN.

Amen.

SACRISTAN.

The end, Father Wardén?

WARDEN.

Aye, surely, brother: are we not always looking out for the Day of judgment?

PROCURATOR.

So said the beloved disciple:—"Little children, it is the last hour; and as you have heard that Antichrist cometh, even now there are many Antichrists; whereby we know that it is the last hour."

BURŞAR.

So, too, said the great Pope, Saint Gregory, more than eight centuries agone.

GUEST-MASTER.

Holy souls have always felt so keenly the miseries of the world, and the lengths of its departure from God, that it has seemed to them, this corrupt earth must soon call down the penal fires from heaven.

WARDEN.

May He, our future Judge, give us grace to live in constant expectation of that awful coming!

KITCHENER.

Amen.

Reader in Theology.

With our loins girded, and lamps burning in our hands.

Sick Friar.

And we ourselves like to men who wait for their Lord: that when He cometh, and knocketh, we may open to him immediately.

Warden.

Saint Francis gives us grace so to wear his cord! better girdle wherewith to meet our Lord at His sudden coming, could not be.

Procurator.

I think you meant something, Father Warden, that more visibly betokened an end, for which we are to prepare. May one ask?

Warden.

Dear brother, is not death near enough, and certain enough? Then, "after death, the judgment." For what are we here, but to prepare for both?

Kitchener.

I, too, thought you saw something more, when you spoke.

WARDEN.

The signs of the times bid me to expect some convulsion, soon or late. There is a spirit abroad, chiefly here in England, though not confined to it, that bodes no good. It may be an old man's fears; but as we near the grave, the earth we are leaving seems more overcast with shadows.

BURSAR.

And the heaven that opens before you, Father Warden, looks the brighter and clearer.

WARDEN.

Much, brother, must be cleansed from the soul before it enters the New Jerusalem, that is of pure gold and precious stones: "into which nothing that is defiled entereth."

GUEST-MASTER.

You spoke, belike, just now, of Wycliffe and his Lollards?

WARDEN.

Of these among others: for "their name is Legion."

SICK FRIAR.

But it is now full seventy years since that false teacher went to his account.

WARDEN.

Alas, when men's bodies die, their deeds live after them.

SUB-WARDEN.

"Some men's sins are manifest, going before to judgment: and some men they follow after."

WARDEN.

The effect of what he taught, and of the countenance given to it by some powerful ones (whom God of His mercy assoil), was plainly shown in the parliament that assembled the year after the heretic's death, as we all remember.

KITCHENER.

Is it not strange, Father Warden, that men with all the experience of past ages,—as that Wycliffe, say, or any other—should not see how the liberties of the Church are linked with the liberties of the subject?

SUB-WARDEN.

Aye, while kings have ever tended to despotism, churchmen have ever stood in the breach against them, for God and the people.

SACRISTAN.

Witness the great Archbishop Langton, who once

and again withstood the tyranny of the impious John. Witness his successors, Winchelsey, ahd the sainted Scroop—

Warden.

Men think not of past ages, brother, even if they know ought about them. They are carried away by the present, by the lust of power, or the greed of wealth. Kings, for their own selfish ambition, or to gratify a private grudge, decree the murther of a vast multitude of their fellows, made to the image of the Maker of all. Then they levy a tax to support their wars, and come down alike upon the widow, the orphan, the labouring man, the consecrated priest.

Sick Friar.

Truly, if the priest dispense not his means to widow, orphan, and labouring man, there may be some show of reason in the procedure.

Sub-Warden.

Nay, brother, neither reason nor right. If the priest be selfish, and indulge in pomp and good cheer,—if he "seek his own, not the things that are Jesus Christ's,"—so much the worse for him: but "to his own Master he standeth or falleth." Human hand may not touch the Ark of God, even when it seemeth to totter.

BURSAR.

What a dread sight is a priest who liveth unmindful of his vocation, and is drowned in the cares or the pleasures of this passing world!

WARDEN.

The priest who misses his vocation becomes a nothing: nay, a nothing is noble, and solid, in comparison of him.

READER IN THEOLOGY.

As saith the prophet: the vine, if it cease to yield fruit to the dresser of the vineyard, becomes unfit for any use, and the most profitless of wood.

PROCURATOR.

And how forcible is Saint Augustine in applying that text! Or the Lord of all the prophets: "Ye are the salt of the earth. But if the salt have lost its savour wherewith shall it be salted? It is thenceforth good for nothing."

KITCHENER.

From the charge of luxury and pomp, at least, we are free, methinks.

WARDEN.

So long as we keep close to the spirit of our Seraphic father. But the storm I speak of wil come, and may involve us all. Even these poor walls may one day be thrown down, stone from stone: and Saint Clare's well be given back to the cattle.

READER IN THEOLOGY.

Though, mostly, it be the taller pinnacle that draweth on itself the lightning.

SUB-WARDEN.

Such inroad would be indeed a fearful sacrilege to the perpetrator. I cannot read over the deed of gift in our archives, by which this spot of earth is ours, and its confirmation by our holy Father from Rome, without trembling for such as may lie under those anathemas in the latter days.

PROCURATOR.

Unhappy souls, if such there are to be! The language of the Psalms, denouncing the enemies of Holy Church, is scarcely more awful. I, too, cannot listen to those deeds read in the refectory on our founder's day, but I seem to hear a distant muttering of thunder on a cloudless summer evening.

WARDEN.

Yet plainly thus to warn is the truest charity: for is not he a friend who calls to the traveller when his foot wanders near the precipice?

INFIRMARIAN.

Even as the Athanasian Creed, that defines what he must believe who would be saved.

SUB-WARDEN.

And as the Church in all her Councils, from Nicæa to Constance, and Basle. Such is her office, and such her mission upon earth. But from what quarter will that storm whereof you speak arise, Father Warden?

WARDEN.

Dear brother, I am no prophet: see for yourself. The nobles of a kingdom, men who are apt to have no perception of what worldly wealth means, but to spend it in hawking and hunting, banquets, and minstrelsy, are thereby prone to look askance at every gold piece in the hand of a churchman. Kings, again, are always needy; for either they are at war, or feasting with expence at home: and in both cases, would gladly own the acres which the piety of former days has left to maintain the daily Sacrifice, and the voice of prayer, throughout the land.

GUEST-MASTER.

And the common folk, Father?

WARDEN.

The folk be our chief friends: they surround our

altars, receive the Sacraments at our hands, and know our lives. Their poorer members are daily relieved at our gate. When sick, they apply to our infirmarian, and are counselled in their difficulties by the first friar they meet. Yet they are fickle, and apt to be led by those above them. Was it not shown, some twenty years back, by the insurrection of the Lollards under him whom men call the Lord Cobham, when throne and altar were threatened alike?

PROCURATOR.

May one enquire, Father Warden, whether your letter from London, which came post to-day, had anything of interest to the Community?

WARDEN.

Little, save that our brethren in the Cornhill are well; and well-loved, to judge by what the Warden tells me of the crowds who seek their ghostly aid. He also writes that their new library, built some eight years since, by Whittyngton, Lord Mayor, is becoming well stocked with books, through the diligence of the brothers in the Scriptorium.

BURSAR.

Good, every way: for idleness is the great gate, without barbican or portcullis, for the devil's entrance into the soul.

WARDEN.

As we move along, I will speak of a Conference even now held at Arras, of which tidings have reached me. May it put an end to that long and bloody war between our country and our neighbour of France!

SUB-WARDEN.

And might it do—what no human conference or treaty can—wipe out the stain left upon our banners by the blood of the hapless Maid of Orleans!

PROCURATOR.

Aye, that was a stain to dim the glories of Agincourt, that were won by fasting and humble prayer—

GREAT BELL.

Toll! toll! toll! toll!

SUB-WARDEN.

The Presence of God!

MASTER OF NOVICES, in the distance.

The Presence of God!

WARDEN.

Aye? so our recreation is half over. My mind was bent on what we spoke of, and I marked not the passage of time.

First Friar.

The English leopard showed himself, indeed, at Rouen, a savage and ruthless beast of prey; and against a guiltless maiden, whom the lion would have spared.

Infirmarian.

She died like a Saint, they say, after living like a heroine.

Procurator.

I had rather wear my grey frock than the rochet of the Bishop of Beauvais—

Warden.

Judge not, that ye be not judged. Let me rather go back to the day of Agincourt. Heard ye, my brethren, of the act of devotion wherewith our countrymen began that great fight?

Sacristan.

Naught especial, Father Warden, if I may answer for the rest.

Warden.

Thus, then, it was. Our poor starved English, with trust, nor hope, in aught but God, in the face of six—some chroniclers say ten—times the number of their enemies, spent the night before, partly in looking to their arms, partly in cleansing their souls by good confession: while the French foeman, exulting in his strength, caroused, and triumphed before the fight was won.

Sick Friar.

No good preparation, that, whether for victory or death.

Warden.

Then, at sunrise, having heard Mass, they advanced the banners of our Lady, St. Edward, and Monseigneur St. George, that good knight: our King in person ranging himself to fight under that of God's blessed Mother. When he advanced in front of his men, and gave the word, "Banners, forward!" then arose a shout from English hearts; and Sir Thomas Erpingham, throwing his baton into the air—

Sub-Warden.

Methinks, I could all but cheer, in memory of that day! Ah, Father Warden, the blood is up in thy veins, that fought on that day!

Warden.

Pardon, my children, pardon! Alas, alas! so it is, in truth: the antient Adam, nay, the antient Cain—

Sub-Warden.

What art thou doing, father? to kneel thus in presence of thy children and subjects!

Warden.

Here on my knees, I crave forgiveness of the Community for my words, too full of the spirit of this world! What hath a Friar Minor, whose mission is to preach "peace on earth, to men of good will"—what hath he to do with such memories as betrayed my sinful heart—

Sub-Warden.

Nay, Father Warden, you wring *all* our hearts. Check not and chapter not yourself thus, in presence of us your children!

Sub-Warden.

Would our Father Provincial were here, to make you rise from off your knees!

Warden.

So, then—proceed we with our recreation. Where was I?

Sick Friar.

Fighting at Agin—

Warden.

Nay, dear brother: I have doffed my hauberk,

and hung up my sword. Yet we will place ourselves in the van, ere the trumpets blow; advanced before the front rank, and beside the priest who stood there—

SACRISTAN.

A priest?

WARDEN.

Even so, and with One greater than himself. A chaplain of our army, vested and stoled, stood there, before the foremost archer or man-at-arms, and raised the adorable Host in sight of all—

SUB-WARDEN.

Heard one ever the like?

WARDEN.

Then each man fell on his knees, and pressed his lips to the ground. "Ha!" we heard a cry from the French ranks: "see! they bite the dust before their time!"

PROCURATOR.

Did our soldiers thus out of humility, Father Warden?

WARDEN.

Humility, brother, and faith beside. They bit

indeed the dust: but it was by taking into their lips, each man, a particle of earth, in token he desired, yet esteemed him unworthy, to receive the Housel that was in sight before them all.

Reader in Theology.

And in one short hour after, many a French lip that had curled in scorn, lay soiled with earth and gore in the pains of death.

Warden.

Brother, forbear—lest the antient enemy bestir him in our hearts again!—See, our novices, with brother Louis, are coming up the alley, in their turn. Ah, pure souls! that have known so little of this vile earth!

Procurator.

Young Didacus, at least, hath known somewhat; and all the more merit for him to quit the world that promised him so fair. They that came back from the bloody fields of our late wars, at Orleans and elsewhere, report him a very lion in the fight.

Warden.

He hath been found by Saint Francis, like other wild animals: like the wolf of Agnani, and that human wolf, who from Lupus was changed into

Agnellus.* Move we down the alley, and give place to the little flock. I hear their joyous bleating. What a gift is religious cheerfulness!

Sick Friar.

They be tuned to the pipe of the gentle shepherd that leadeth them.

Warden.

Walk we too briskly for you, dear brother?

Sick Friar.

Nay, Father Warden, old limbs are the better for this movement: so let us on—

Master of Novices.

Come, as we are speaking of tombs and epitaphs, I will tell you of one lately inscribed on a monument in Mailross Abbey, the house of the great Cuthbert; which expresseth much in a few words. It is not so terse as the one you quoted, Felix: but then, we must make allowance for a poet, who will have his say. Thus it runs:

> "Earth walketh on the earth,
> Glistering like gold,
> Earth goeth to the earth
> Sooner than it wold.

* "Saint Francis and the Franciscans," pp. 186, 187.

> Earth buildeth on the earth
> Palaces and towers:
> Earth sayeth to the earth,
> All shall be ours!"

What think you of it, my children? Antony, how say you?

ANTONY.

Why father, if I had had the misfortune to die in the world, I had rather they engraved a short petition on my tomb-stone, to remind charitable Christians to pray for my soul. Such verses as these might have been written even by Horace, who says—

DIDACUS.

Now we shall have another quotation.

ANTONY.

I forgot. But, for instance: I had rather it ran,

> "Such a one—such a one—*gist icy:*
> *Dieu de sa alme ayt mercy!*

There is some comfort about that.

PACIFICUS.

Or, shorter still, "*Cujus aæ pcietur Deus;*" with the letters all crumpled up, as if the stone-cutter was to get a *Miserere* discipline for every additional stroke he made.

Master of Novices.

They would be less chary of their letters and words, in books, if not on stones, could they discover some art of producing many copies of a manuscript without writing it all over again each time. I have often pondered over some words of our great brother—now, I trust with God—Roger. Bacon, which look that way. I see not wherefore it might not be done.

Felix.

What would then become of our Scriptorium?

Agnellus.

No more red and blue dragons with whirligig tails from Brother Antony.

Silvester.

No more butterflies, apes, and strawberries.

Didacus.

Unless they, too, were impressed on the parchment.

Master of Novices.

Thomas, a penny for your thoughts, if it be not against poverty. What art musing upon?

Thomas.

Am I to make an act of simplicity, Father, and tell it out straight?

Master of Novices.

Out with it—the straighter the better.

Thomas.

Why, those verses, all about earth, kept jingling in my ears, till I found my thoughts running into rhymes, too, such as they are.

All the Novices.

Oh, let us have them!

Master of Novices.

Rivalling your namesake, Thomas the Rhymer. Well? Is it anything like Antony's favourite Latin poets?

"*Nos, ubi decidimus,
Pulvis et umbra sumus?*"

Thomas.

Nay, neither Virgil, nor Horace would own them. But here they are, for better, for worse:—

"Earth from the earth shall rise
  Unearthly fair:
If earth do earth despise
  And what is there.
But when earth earth does love,
  Earthy earth grows:
Such earthly earth above
  Ne'er from earth rose!"

MASTER OF NOVICES.

Well, they may be called an expansion of that dictum of S. Augustine I told you of, not long ago. "Each man resembles that which he loves:—if thou lovest earth, then earth thou art." At least, they will find their place among such verses as may be called "well-meaning."

THOMAS.

I am content with that praise, Father.

MASTER OF NOVICES.

You have reason, my dear son. Happy were it for many a poetaster, aye, and for many a man with the true poetic fire, if his productions were as harmless as this, which will not put Saint Clare's well in any danger of conflagration.

DIDACUS.

More innocent than those of one Sir Geoffrey Chaucer, which I heard before I left the world.

MASTER OF NOVICES.

Leave Chaucer also, my son, and forget him. I fear me, like others before him, he has had much to answer for, in many ways. But as he has written things that are like to draw men away from the law of the Lord, it is of less moment that he may also have written lightly about the frock of the Friar Minor.

PACIFICUS.

May we make a memento for him at Mass tomorrow, Father?

MASTER OF NOVICES.

We will all do so, and at Matins to-night. That is the best return for his hard speeches. "Pray for them that persecute and calumniate you: that you may be the children of your Father who is in heaven."

ANTONY.

Ah, what inward pleasure does that give to the heart: even should it do no outward good to the subject of the prayer.

MASTER OF NOVICES.

Alas, poor soul! five and thirty full years hath he now been in the other world: and who shall know, or guess, in what state? I trust he may have had a zealous ghostly father at the last, and made a perfect shrift. But he more than half cast in his lot with the Lollards: I know not who could absolve him. I never heard he recanted. God knows; may He at that moment have seen somewhat in his favour.

FELIX.

Five and thirty years! what must be five and thirty moments, to a soul that now perceives what it is to possess God, yet finds itself—even for awhile—debarred from Him!

ANTONY.

From the sight and possession of Him!

PACIFICUS.

From the ecstatic enjoyment of Him!

AGNELLUS.

And, in Him, of all things!

DIDACUS.

What, then, if for ever?

MASTER OF NOVICES.

Be we therefore zealous, "while we have time."

GREAT BELL.

Toll! toll! toll! toll! toll! toll! toll! toll!

MASTER OF NOVICES.

Everything prepared for Vespers? let us go in.

The Seven Ages of Clarewell.

AGE THE FOURTH: 1536.

DISSOLVED.

(CLOISTER, WITHIN THE INNER GATE).

Warden.

Hasten, then, Brother Masseo; bar the outer gate! What would you say to me, my children?

Miller.

Reverend Father Warden, here be Gregory, myself, my two sons, and half a score of stout lads beside: we pray you, let us man the gate-house with our arblasts and long-bows. I warrant you, we'll keep them at bay.

Warden.

No, my son: not an arrow shall be shot, nor a stroke dealt, in this place. The house of God is not to be held by force of arms, like a baron's castle.

AGE THE FOURTH—DISSOLVED.

MILLER.

But these caitiffs will soon break through the gate, if no defence be made: and what happens then?

WARDEN.

Brother Juniper, since the evil day has come upon us, take with you two or three of those good fellows; go straight to the Sub-Warden. Ye will find him in his cell. Let him take our deed of gift, and the other charters by which we hold our lands—

MILLER.

What a pother they do keep outside!

WARDEN.

Go with him to the choir, in all haste—unscrew the ball of the brass eagle from which the lections are wont to be chanted—

PURSUIVANT (from without).

Open! in the King's name!

WARDEN.

Bestow the parchments safely within it; screw the ball tight, so to resist the water, all it may:—then drag the eagle forth—fling it into the fish-pond, and mark well the spot! It may abide better days. Away! fail not—delay not—

PURSUIVANT.

In the King's name, I say, ye traitors!

MILLER.

How say you, Brother Antony, up there? what see you through the window?

LAY-BROTHER.

They have brought up a beam; a heavy one. Now they swing it on, by a chain, to a large tressle. Five or six men are ready to launch it against the gate! Ha!

MILLER.

Hark, there go the strokes! and there, again!

LAY-BROTHER.

They will soon have the gate in, at this rate!

GREGORY.

Nay, Father Warden, we beseech you—

MILLER'S SON.

It is our common cause: the friary is the apple of our eye—

LAY-BROTHER.

There, again! a stroke that would break into Nottingham Castle—the gate is well nigh off its hinges.

WARDEN.

I will go to them, and hold a parley—

MILLER.

Would I could stay you, Reverend Father: these villains have no more respect for the cowl than Saint Thomas met in his own Church at Canterbury!

WARDEN.

A good remembrance, for which I thank thee. 'Twas even that holy martyr who forbade the church doors to be closed against his murderers—"The good shepherd giveth his life for the sheep." Come with me, Masseo, and unbar the wicket.

LAY-BROTHER.

Ha! that last stroke saves all trouble: the gate is down!

WARDEN.

Open the inner gate: we are overcome by force. I make appeal to right, if any be left in England:—if not, then to Rome, the mother of us all.

Pursuivant.

Open, in the King's name! Soh! here we are: a poorish place, after all.

Man-at-Arms.

Trouble enough ye gave us, ye shavelings, with your old gate. 'Tis well this second one was not defended! for when one's blood's up—

Warden.

Peace! ye are in. What would ye more? what is your errand?

Dr. Lee.*

Read the commission, Pursuivant.

Pursuivant.

"Whereas, by authority of our Sovereign Lord the King, we, Thomas Cromwell, have been appointed the royal vicegerent, vicar-general, and principal commissary, with all the spiritual authority belonging to the King as head of the Church, for the due administration of justice in all cases touching the ecclesiastical jurisdiction, and the godly reformation and redress of all errors, heresies, and abuses in the said Church"—

---

* One of the Royal Commissioners for the Visitation of Monasteries: Lingard, vol. V, pp. 54, 98, *notes*. For the Commission, Ibid. p. 51.

WARDEN.

Enough, enough. Thus far have we listened, out of respect for the name of the King's grace, that stands at the head of thy parchment. For this same Thomas Cromwell, we know him not.

LEE.

Therein, as in all else, are ye behind the times. Our sovereign hath made the Lord Cromwell all which he here describeth himself to be: in Parliament, he sitteth before the Archbishop of Canterbury, and supersedeth him likewise as the president of Convocation.

WARDEN.

A chief place in Parliament my sovereign may bestow on whomsoever he will: but a spiritual authority is not his to give to mortal man; nor, in sooth, to take away.

LEE.

How now, traitor?

PURSUIVANT.

Dost thou deny the King to be supreme head of the Church?

LEE.

Beware: or we shall write thee down on the same

headless list with the traitor More, who must needs boggle about that oath, a year since, till they left him never a tongue to wag on it:—

PURSUIVANT.

And my Lord of Rochester,* ha! to whom the Pope would have sent a hat, but that the King's grace relieved him of the head that should wear it.

LEE.

How, now, about the supreme power, ye knaves? and the King's marriage with the Lady Anne?

WARDEN.

Truly, Master Lee, thus much—I hope—is safe to affirm: they be evil days in England, when one must give a new head to the Church, or lose one's own.

SUB-WARDEN.

Father Warden, stay, I pray thee; fall not into the trap this artful man hath set for thee.

* The saintly and martyred Fisher, Bishop of Rochester, one of the counsellors of the late King During the long and rigorous confinement he underwent in the Tower, Pope Paul III. signified his intention of bestowing on him the purple: to which Henry VIII. made the brutal rejoinder: "Paul may send him a hat, but I will leave him never a head to set it on!"

SACRISTAN.

Be we wise as serpents, and harmless as doves.

LEE.

Nay, but an answer we will have: for our commission stretches so far as to examine and apprehend all person or persons suspected of treason, friar or layman alike.

WARDEN.

This is my answer: I hope you bow to the authority whence it comes. I desire to "render to Cæsar the things that are Cæsar's, and to God the things that are God's."

LEE.

Aye, we know how you can slip out of a plain question.

SUB-WARDEN.

When the answer means, all the butcheries of Tyburn, one had well need—

LEE.

How make ye this ado, ye knaves, when other houses, yea, of your own Order, have come to reason, and made their submission to the King?

WARDEN.

Nay, Master Lee, that may I scarce believe. Our brethren are not fallen so low.

LEE.

I come straight from Brentingham, and have their deed of surrender even now in my mails. Nay, here is it, in my pouch.

SUB-WARDEN.

Brentingham is a house whereinto one of the Lords of Council, they say, prevailed to force a secular Canon as Warden, a boon companion of his own. Would you set before us such a man for an ensample?

WARDEN.

My son, let us speak ill of no man. It is nothing to us, but grief only, if all the Grey friars' houses in England have wittingly given in their names to this ungodly thing.

LEE.

Listen to their words,* and be ye ruled to do the like.

"Forasmuch as we, the Warden and Friars of the house of Saint Francis in Brentingham, com-

---

* See Dugdale, vol. VIII, p. 1534.

monly called the Grey Friars, do profoundly consider that the perfection of Christian living doth not consist in dumb ceremonies"—

WARDEN.

Nay, this is no mere surrender, but heresy to boot. Every Christian doth reverence to the ceremonies of the Church; and a monk or friar to those of his order; and he that—

LEE.

"Nor in wearing of a grey coat, disguising ourselves after strange fashions"—

SACRISTAN.

Heard one ever so manifest a perversion of a plain matter?

LEE.

"Ducking, nodding, and becking"—

INFIRMARIAN.

A stiff-necked generation!

BURSAR.

That bends the knee to Mammon only.

PURSUIVANT.

Silence, sirs, we shall come to that part of the business presently—

LEE.

"Girding ourselves with a girdle full of knots, and other like Papistical ceremonies, wherein we had been most principally practised and misled in times past"—

BROTHER JUNIPER.

A word in your ear, Reverend Father:—the eagle, with the parchments inside it, is safe in the fish-pond; I marvel they heard not the splash!

PURSUIVANT.

What treason are they hatching there together? Sirrah soldier, secure yon froward old friar, and bind him. Where be the cords you brought with you?

WARDEN.

Be content: he shall not interrupt again. And for us, spare us all that length of words.

SUB-WARDEN.

Such things we know, or guess at.

WARDEN.

We are not ignorant of your doings, and those of Master Layton, in other of the shires of England; nor how much the fear of the world hath here and there unhappily prevailed over the constancy which a religious man owes to his Rule, and to the Lord who hath laid it on him.

PROCURATOR.

Neither pleasure is it, nor advantage to us, to hear how some among our brethren have left their first love, and fallen into grievous sin.

PURSUIVANT.

It would be your advantage, methinks, ye naughty friars, to be counselled to escape the knife and halter at Tyburn!

WARDEN.

Not so: for "what shall a man give in exchange for his soul?"

LEE.

There is a nearer way, sirrah Warden: we will even tie you up in one of your own corn sacks, and throw you into that Clare's Well, whereof men hereabout speak so much.

MAN-AT-ARMS.

'Twould be beyond its power of working wonders, to cause a friar, with a stone around his neck, to rise again to the top, like a cork.

WARDEN.

Threaten them that are in love with life. For us,

by the help of God to our unworthiness, "for the sake of the words of His lips, we have kept hard ways."* A moment of drowning in the well of Saint Clare is light, when set against a week of observance in the house called by her name.

PURSUIVANT.

They are as obstinate as their own swine. Try them with the promises we are commissioned to hold out—

LEE.

Hear, then, ye varlets, the grace of our lord the King. After your froward speeches, it goeth against one to give you such easy terms: notwithstanding, hear ye—

WARDEN.

Mistake not our speeches, nor our spirit. The Grey friars, as their bounden duty is, have ever been loyal to their King. Have ye not read in the Chronicle, how Brother Richard Friseley, the Warden of our house in Leicester, was condemned, drawn, and hanged in his religious habit and weed, for believing and asserting that King Richard the Second was yet alive? how, shortly after, and on the same cause, two friars of his house in that town, and eight in London, were hanged and beheaded—

* Psalm xvi. 5.

LEE.

Waste not the time with unprofitable speech, but rather hear and accept the King's bounty that now is—

PURSUIVANT.

Whom God long preserve!

WARDEN AND THE REST.

Amen, and amen.

SUB-WARDEN.

God save the King!

PROCURATOR.

Save him from evil counsellors, and from the Enemy of us all.

LEE.

Our sovereign lord, King Henry the Eighth, Prince of England, France, and Ireland, taking into his princely consideration—

WARDEN.

Master Lee, we pray you, to shorten the rehearsal of all we acknowledge, as loyal liege subjects, and tell us what our King demandeth of us.

LEE.

He demandeth the surrender of the house and

lands which ye have forfeited by your evil living, together with the mill, dove-cote, messuages, ox-gangs, garths, and closes, the carucates, marshes, and other advantages—

WARDEN.

One answer sufficeth for all. We render to Cæsar—

SUB-WARDEN.

Dear Father Warden, respect your grey hairs, and do not, where no need is—

LEE.

Let him proceed: it is but of a piece with the rest, ye shavelings. I marvel, his Grace hath not ere now suppressed you, together with your other houses of cordeliers, that must needs range yourselves, forsooth, on the part of the late Queen—

WARDEN.

Late Queen? "what God hath joined, let no man put asunder." Who shall declare that marriage void, if he doth not, to whom was given power to bind and to loose on earth?

LEE.

Stand aside, that we may do our errand. It resteth with you, my masters, to make your peace with the King's grace, and surrender in all quietness.

WARDEN.

Whatsoever were lawfully our own, did we possess aught, we would surrender, as compelled, if even not of good will: here we be stewards only, and in trust for them that come after us, as well as for them that went before.

PURSUIVANT.

That went before, forsooth!—and what have they to say to it?

WARDEN.

Have ye so far left your faith, that ye have no pity on the souls of such as founded a perpetual dole to the poor at our gates, and masses to be said for ever at our altars, for the needs wherein they perchance suffer, even now, and cannot help their ownselves?

LEE.

We come not here to chop logic, nor to dispute divinity. My masters, all, hear ye. We lay not to your charge the frowardness of them that have ruled you even to this day. We proclaim to you the grace of our lord the King: that such of you as will, may retire to the larger houses of your Order, wherein, as the late Act of Parliament affirmeth,* "thanks be to God, religion is right well observed and kept up"—

Procurator.

Tell that tale to the children in the nighest grammar-school!

Bursar.

A likely thing, forsooth, that religion should there most flourish where is greatest danger from the world, the flesh, and the devil—

Reader in Theology.

Where the alms of the faithful have so abounded, as it needeth the more fasting and prayer to save the house from the concupiscence of the eyes, and the pride of life—

Pursuivant.

Oyez, oyez, oyez!

Lee.

Or further, an ye list, ye may return to the world, to work, like sturdy knaves, for your bread; even as our first father Adam, who delved, while Eve span—

* 27 Henry VIII. c. 28, for suppressing the lesser monasteries.

SUB-WARDEN.

When he was turned out of Paradise—

GUEST-MASTER.

For breaking his Rule, not for keeping it—

LEE.

With a present from the King's bounty of forty shillings current of the realm, and a gown of woollen stuff against the coming winter. And now, what say you?

PURSUIVANT.

All dumb?

ELIAS.

Father Warden, I incline to accept these conditions of our lord the King.

SUB-WARDEN.

Dear brother, take back that word.

SACRISTAN.

Suffer us to think it spoken in jest: though this be, in truth, no jesting season.

ELIAS.

I jest not, I. "Let every one abound in his own sense." Be ye martyrs, an ye will. For me, I have long time thought, albeit I have known how to hold my peace—

PROCURATOR.

It surpriseth me not; and yet, alack the day!

WARDEN.

Alas, alas!

ELIAS.

Our brethren of Brentingham have set forth, in fair phrase, what I, too, feel. 'Tis not the cord, nor strange cowl and attire, nor duckings and noddings, that make a Christian man's acceptableness—

SUB-WARDEN.

Unhappy man! your vows?

ELIAS.

The Lord Cromwell can release me: can he not, Master Lee?

LEE.

Assuredly: wherefore else holdeth he so high an office under the King's grace?

WARDEN.

The vows you did pronounce, after long trial had, with much study and practice of the matter thereof: no man compelling you, yea, some of the Community misdoubting you, who pleaded for a delay you would not hear of—

ELIAS.

Favete linguis: enough said. Henceforth I am free. Master Lee, tender me the Oath. Is it to declare the King supreme head, or that my past life hath been misled, or against Luther and his consubstantiation, or what is it? Anything that cometh to hand, so I be free.

LEE.

It shall suffice for the present to receive your declaration. Stand aside, and proceed we with the rest.

ELIAS.

Stand aside? these be brief commendations. Methought surely you would take down my name, with the heads of what I have said in devotion to my King.

GUEST-MASTER.

This is ever the fate of apostates; to lose both worlds alike. They be contemned by them for whose favour they sell themselves, as they will also be, when the darnel and cockle are bound in bundles for the burning.

LEE.

Silence, fellow; and take heed to thyself. We shall not recommend *thee* for the forty shillings and gown of woollen stuff.

GUEST-MASTER.

Saint Francis be praised therefore.

LEE.

Meanwhile, we are to proffer you all, on the part of his Grace, the fair and clement terms aforesaid. I must needs shorten the business, and away. Who among the elder ones accepteth?

PURSUIVANT.

Oyez—oyez—oyez!

LEE.

This silence breathes contumacy. Once again, Pursuivant.

PURSUIVANT.

Oyez—oyez—oyez!

WARDEN.

Spare yourselves further pains. Among the twelve, was one Judas found. I would fain hope, we have seen the beginning and the ending of such miseries among us here.

ELIAS.

Warden, I warn thee; another word, and I report to his Grace's Council in London full many a speech that hath passed in these walls.

LEE.

What, against the supreme headship?

ELIAS.

Nay, Master Lee, I can keep counsel, even as another. For what said Sampson to the Philistines? "If you had not ploughed with my heifer, you had not found out my riddle." You rob me not, so please you, of proofs that may yet advance me at court.

MAN-AT-ARMS.

Truly, a mean and despicable fellow. This business goeth clean against my conscience. But what can a simple man do, in these times? I like not to be shortened of my stature by a head—

LEE.

What art mumbling over, caitiff?

MAN-AT-ARMS.

Though perchance it were the better for me at the gate of Paradise, which they say requireth both stooping and striving.

SUB-WARDEN.

My son, if anything toucheth thee in the conscience, allow it good room to work: for "what shall a man give in exchange for his soul?"

LEE.

Silence, all. I turn me to the younger ones, who have leave to depart, neither more nor less. Their age, being under twenty-four years, giveth them advantage to strike into less profitless lines of life. How say you, good fellows? will any of you take the King's badge, and serve among the yeomen of the guard? Here be thews and sinews among you that would not discredit the livery. Ha! the life at Greenwich is a jolly life!

WARDEN.

They "walk by faith, not by sight."

NOVICE-MASTER.

And, for threatenings, carry them elsewhere. Our little ones of the flock, even as the faithful kindred of Moses, "feared not the King's edict."

LEE.

Joustings, pel-quintain, quarter-staff by day: always within reach of a butt of ale—

NOVICE-MASTER.

"Choosing rather to suffer persecution with the people of God, than to have the pleasure of sin for a season"—

LEE.

Plenty of broad pieces flying about, stamped with the King's countenance—

NOVICE-MASTER.

"Esteeming the reproach of Christ greater riches than the treasure of the Egyptians"—

LEE.

Dicing and shovelboard; masques, banquettings, and minstrelsy—

NOVICE-MASTER.

"He looked unto the reward."

LEE.

The favour of your King, whose sunshine of his countenance is as dazzling as his wrath is terrible—

NOVICE-MASTER.

"By faith Moses left Egypt, not fearing the fierceness of the King: for he endured, as seeing Him who is invisible."

Lee.

Securing yourselves against misprision of treason, with all that ensueth thereupon.

Novice-Master.

"In nothing terrified by the adversaries; which to them is a cause of perdition, but to you of salvation, and this from God. For to you it is given, for Christ, not only to believe in Him, but also to suffer for His sake."

Warden.

Dear brother, ye are as ready with your texts as a gospeller from Geneva. And you, Master Lee, perceive you that you prevail nothing?

Lee.

Obstinate are ye, even as the beast whereon Balaam rode. Ha! see ye that I also can quote?

Reader in Theology.

Even so it is written in the Gospel, that the Enemy of man, in the wilderness of temptation—

Warden.

Brother, it is written also, though by a human sage, that speech is silver, but silence is gold. Suppose we, then, the bell to have rung for silence, without further answer to these unlooked for guests.

LEE.

Sith ye reject such gracious offers, lo, we exercise the extremity of our commission, and demand of you the surrender of your church and cloister-buildings, together with the closes and parcels or ground adjoining; the tenements, messuages, oxgangs, vineyards, aforesaid—

SUB-WARDEN.

In brief, all we possess; for why dally with words?

WARDEN.

All, of which the piety of former times hath put us in trust. Cæsar hath the power: or Herod, of Pilate—arrange the titles as ye will—

LEE.

Titles, ye traitors, again? Head of the Church, I say; and Defender of the Faith.

READER IN THEOLOGY.

Methinks, both titles were hardly drawn out from the same well.

LEE.

First, surrender ye up to the King the title-deeds, and whatsoever charters they be, whereby ye pretend to hold this place. Then shall ye practise that poverty ye have hitherto pretended.

PROCURATOR.

Pretended, Master Lee? I pray you, look around you. Would it please you to dwell within bare walls, and be served on wooden platters?

BURSAR.

While ye sate in a rude frock, withouten hose?

SICK FRIAR.

Hearkening to the Scriptures, and the Martyrology?

WARDEN.

Your demand lieth not within our compass; the deeds being not to be found on English land.

LAY-BROTHER.

True enough is that same word.

PURSUIVANT.

How mean ye? have ye sent them beyond seas?

LAY-BROTHER.

They have been stowed aboard the good ship " Eagle."

Pursuivant.

And sent afloat?

Lay-Brother.

An they sank not to the bottom.

Warden.

Brother, peace: and you, sirs, content you. The deeds are not in our hands.

Lee.

Will you swear it on the Gospels?

Warden.

The word of a Friar Minor should be as good as his oath. It is even as I say. Copies there are, that were written out some years back: these you can have, or hear them read.

Lee.

Sith better may not be, let the copies be brought forth.

Warden.

Dear brother, bring them forth and read them.

Sub-Warden.

Hearken to the tenor of the deed whereby that noble Knight Sir Humphrey de Mandeville, lord of—

Lee.

Briefly, let his titles be; and, for his goodness, it is enough for you that he founded a Franciscan house, which would in your eyes canonise a lawyer.

Man-at-Arms.

Aye, Master Rich himself, the King's Attorney.

Sub-Warden.

I will recite but the conclusion of his deed of gift, for that it behoveth you much to hear.

Lee.

Read on, and delay not.

Sub-Warden.

"Wherefore, on the part of Almighty God and on mine own, I give strict charge that none of my successors, dependants, or any other, shall presume in anywise to vex nor to molest the aforesaid Convent of Saint Francis, of Clare's Well, commonly called Clarewelle, nor the brethren who serve the divine offices in that place, with respect to such churches or tenements as are afore rehearsed. But should any of them presume in anywise to do or design aught against this my charter, and to alienate this my alms-deed from the aforesaid Convent, or in any respect to diminish the same, let him, in the life that now is, feel the malediction of Almighty God, and of Holy Mary, and of blessed Francis, and of all the Saints of God; and in the life to come, receive eternal damnation with the traitor Judas: unless he repent and amend. So be it.—. So be it. Amen."

LEE.

So be it: let your terrors affect such as they may concern. For us, we act under commission of the Great Seal.

WARDEN.

And we, under that of the King of kings. Come, my brethren, bend we for awhile beneath this storm: for it is written: "When they persecute you in one city, flee ye to another." And, as saith holy Athanasius, that unshaken pillar of the Church, in his *Apologia de fugâ suâ*—

LEE.

Depart, without more ado: and think it well that ye scape thus free, for all your evil words. In the King's name we now take possession. Pursuivant, and you, fellow, see that nothing be taken forth of the house.

WARDEN.

Fiat voluntas tua, sicut in cælo, et in terrâ.

Lee.

Now, good fellows, ye that stand by with mouths agape, will ye earn an honest penny by helping this godly work?

Miller.

Had it not been for their commands whom ye drive hence, we had earned the merit of sending a quarrel* into your right eye.

Gregory.

Ye are bounden to their teaching, which alone hinders us to raise the lads of the village, and scourge you back on your road to London.

Pursuivant.

Dolts that we were, to come with no greater following, and give to such *outrecedance* its meed!

Lee.

Forth with your stubborn selves, and yield place to those we have brought with us.

Warden.

Master Lee, and you, Pursuivant, list ye these my last words, as though the words of a dying man. I would speak them with a coil of Tyburn rope

---

* A shaft, square-headed, (whence its name) shot from the arblast, or cross-bow.

around my neck, and the hangman's knife at my heart. Ye take from God His house, to bestow it on man. He knoweth how to avenge His own cause, and will bestow on man a vengeance worthy of God. "There shall not be an old man in this house for ever:" neither shall these acres, nor the ruins ye leave on this spot, pass from father to son, while time shall be. Fire and water, that serve alike His bidding, shall join in league against the spoiler: and—

LEE.

Away with the dotard!

WARDEN.

Be ye warned, and they that sent you. We have delivered our souls. Come, my brethren, go we forth in the spirit of Saint Francis, and by the words of his Master and ours, taking no scrip for our journey, nor two coats, nor shoes, nor a staff—

LEE.

First, bid two or three stout fellows mount to yonder bell turret, and cast down the bell. Sooth to say, it hath been won at dice* by some who press to have it converted into money at the soonest.

* So Sir Miles Partridge afterwards won, at a cast of dice played with Henry VIII., a peal of bells called "Jesus' bells," "hanging in a steeple not far from St. Paul's, London, very remarkable both for their size and music." Stow's Survey of London, apud Collier, ii. 166.

WARDEN.

Let us form in Choir, for the last time within these old walls, that have sheltered some of us even from our boyhood, and all from the moment when Grace called louder than the world. As the swan dies in song, so shall Clarewell be dissolved amid the praises of the Lord.

MEN IN THE TOWER.

Hack!—hack!—hack!

WARDEN.

Intone we the psalm, *Deus, venerunt gentes:* and so make an end. Thanks be to God, that the Housel was consumed this morning, and our relics safely bestowed.

LEE.

See that some be ready presently to strip the lead off the roof.

MILLER.

Is it in flesh and blood to stand this? how say you, Gregory?

MEN IN THE TOWER.

Hack!—hack!—hack!

GREGORY.

I am ready, an thou art: and dare as much for Saint Francis.

WARDEN.

Dear friends and children, I bid you, peace! Go ye forth before us. Nay, in your eyes, it is our own house still. Go we all forth together, in God's name.

MEN IN THE TOWER.

Hack!—hack!—hack!

WARDEN.

"*Deus, venerunt gentes.* O God! the heathen are come into Thine inheritance"—

CHOIR OF FRIARS.

"They have defiled Thy holy temple: they have made Jerusalem as a place to keep fruit."

MILLER.

Hush, then, Gregory—tread we silently forth, at head of the procession. Here comes the cross. Come, lads, and make no ado, since 'tis the father's will.

MEN IN THE TOWER.

Hack!—hack!—hack!

MILLER'S SON.

I would I had licence with my quarter-staff a brief space!

MILLER.

Quarter-staff, Wat? nay, with licence, naught should content a man of us but sword and buckler!

WARDEN.

"We are become a reproach to our neighbours:"

CHOIR.

"A scorn and a derision to them that are round about us."

MEN IN THE TOWER.

Hack!—hack!—hack!

WARDEN.

"They have devoured Jacob:"

CHOIR.

"And have laid waste his place."

WARDEN.

"Remember not our former iniquities:"

CHOIR.

"Let Thy mercies speedily prevent us, for we are becoming exceeding poor."

MEN IN THE TOWER.

Hack!—hack!—hack!—hack!

AGE THE FOURTH—DISSOLVED.

WARDEN.

"Help us, O God our Saviour:"

CHOIR.

"And for the glory of Thy name, O Lord! deliver us: and forgive us our sins for Thy name's sake!"

WARDEN.

"Lest they should say among the Gentiles"—

MEN IN THE TOWER.

Hack!—hack!

GREAT BELL, *falling*.

Toll! Clang! Crash!

The Seven Ages of Clarewell.

AGE THE FIFTH: 1636.

SECULARISED.

(THE CHAPTER-HOUSE, FITTED UP AS A WITH-DRAWING ROOM. A MULLIONED WINDOW LOOKING ON THE GARDEN.)

SIR HENRY SPELMAN.

After my humble duty to your ladyship, my first care is to advise you wherefore I have so far presumed as to ask two friends, strangers to yourself, to meet me even in your house. A freedom which, as it is clean foreign to my habits, so—

DAME CURETON.

Your antient friendship, Sir Henry, with my deceased lord, would excuse this, and more: my poor house is at your command. Besides, that the name of Master Dugdale is not unknown to me; he is, in truth, a distant Warwickshire kinsman, and welcome for his own sake, as for yours. Howbeit, I trust these gentlemen, both, will pardon my absence from your interview. Widowhood, and that lowness of spirits against which I may but poorly strive—

SPELMAN.

Say no more, mine honoured lady and hostess. Do but entrust to me the entertainment of these friends; I warrant they shall not depart ill-content with the hospitality of Clarewell. Both, indeed, are men retired and studious in their habits, not given to those roystering libations which are among the plague-spots of our evil times.

THE DAME.

We know Sir Henry Spelman for a praiser of past days, by comparison of those that now are. Yet, could we believe some of those same roysterers, whose sallies and songs have rung, in sooth too loudly, under these roof-trees, in years gone by, then the vineyards here, whose old stumps yet remain in the pleasaunce, were not only for the altar when Clarewell was a friary.

SPELMAN.

Lady, it is not you, methinks, nor they whose prayer-books are so well worn as yours, that would lightly credit what ribald wits and profane songsters might vent against men whose lives they comprehend not. Their calumnies were winged by that hate which cometh not from the injured, but the injurer.

The Dame.

Good sooth, mine antient friend, you have harped, all on a sudden, upon a string to which my heart responds, yea, even too readily. It is not always the light word betokens the light thought.

Spelman.

True: but what said I?

The Dame.

Often, and of late more strongly, is it borne in upon my mind, perchance the misfortunes thou knowest to have gathered round our house, came upon me and mine, forasmuch as we have stepped —aye, intruded, into a place—

Spelman.

Nay, madam, I desired not to prompt such a thought. Let me rather tell you who is the other guest I am momently expecting.

The Dame.

I should have asked, ere now: your chance word put all else from my thoughts.

Spelman.

'Tis one Master Roger Dodsworth, a gentleman of a good family in Yorkshire, whose studies, like those of his senior, Master Dugdale, have lain principally among antient deeds and charters, that speak to us in such lively sort of the spirit and convictions of the men of old.

The Dame.

Truly, their voice is living still! "being dead, they yet speak."

Spelman.

And with no foreign accent. They were bone of our bone, and flesh of our flesh: Englishmen, and one with us, in all but that religion, whereof, I confess, the more I read, the more in its effects do I admire it.

Sewer.

Madam, may it please you to command some refection for the guests who are waited for?

The Dame.

A flask of Tokay, good Wallis, and the tall Venetian glasses thereunto, with a manchet of fine bread, stewed quinces and medlars, on a napkin of fine damask, until John Cook's knife shall sound on the dresser.

Sewer.

It shall be done, madam.

The Dame.

To me, those voices sound severely, as bearing a reproach: ah, me! they weigh upon my heart—and, as they closed the future, they seem to interpret the past.

Spelman.

Speak you in general, lady, or is there more meaning in your words?

The Dame.

I will impart it to you, out of the antient love that was betwixt yourself and my lord that is gone. Take but the pains to move toward yonder cabinet: open the third drawer from the top—nay, good sir, there, on your left hand—so.

Spelman.

What have we here? a crumpled packet of antient parchments, that hath lain, methinks, in the water, and is half spoiled. They be musty enough for a score of Dugdales, and Dodsworths to boot.

The Dame.

Even so: parchment deeds are they, and of antient date. Some eight years agone, my lord would employ his knaves that were idle, and gave them far a task to draw off the fish-ponds in the pleasaunce. You have tasted of our carp, Sir Henry, and have heard him say, he thanked the friars of old for ponds and fishes alike.

SPELMAN.

You bring to mind, indeed, many a peaceful day of recreation here.

THE DAME.

Ah, so! Grace be given us to win through the remainder of our pilgrimage: for "the time is short."

SPELMAN.

But the pond, and the parchments?

THE DAME.

The water being drained away by lifting of the penstock, there was found, not only great sight of carp of a huge bigness, that might have been fed—or their immediate ancestors—by the hands of the Clarewell friars, but a marvellous thing indeed, beside.

SPELMAN.

I am fain to guess, but cannot.

THE DAME.

Bedded in the mud, and near the brink of the

pond, lay an antient brass eagle, such as we yet behold in our large minsters and college churches, with half-spread wings.

Spelman.

A thing, indeed, quite out of the common way, to be thus found; and one that will be welcome to Master Dugdale to hear of.

The Dame.

The marvel is yet to come. While they dragged this over-rusted eagle to land, the globe of brass whereon the talons rested was found to loosen in the midst, which caused them to look curiously on it, and try it, till they perceived it to be so fashioned as to unscrew: and thus, opening the ball, they discovered these parchments bestowed in the hollow thereof.

Spelman.

Truly, that surpasseth. The friars had doubtless so hid them away, an hundred years back, hoping the storm would pass; and so by aid of these title-deeds they might once again recover their lands and tenements.

The Dame.

There, my friend, lieth the ground of my anxious thoughts; and so will you perceive when you shall have read them over. You know my past misfortunes, and those of my late lord—yea, and of his great uncle before him: how that strange and sudden deaths, and—sooth to say—great crimes as well as sorrows—

Spelman.

Madam, I pray of you, spare yourself: it has been my lot, not twice nor thrice. to administer such comfort as I might, within these walls, when dark thoughts pressed heavily—

The Dame.

Right well I know it: and from you, Sir Henry, such comfort cometh with power; since you, of all men, know the full meaning of the word that accounteth for all: one of the darkest, methinks, in our cheerful English tongue.

Spelman.

The word, lady?

The Dame.

Are ye, then, grown so dull on a sudden? Men say, you are plunged in such studies as are concerned with that very phrase, and will one day give them to the world. Pause you still? the word is *Sacrilege.*

Spelman.

Mine honoured friend, how shall I make answer? I trust, the Eye that surveys all things from the supreme height, marketh well a difference between them that of themselves have snatched, and them that have but received.

The Dame.

"You cram these words into mine ear," as Will Shakspeare hath it, against my better sense—nay, and against your own notings down of what chanceth on every side. Even human law counts the receiver as partner in the guilt. No wonder is it to see the eagle's nest on fire, when she hath caught up a brand with the dedicated flesh meats on the altar, to feed therewith her young.

Spelman.

Yet the eaglets were guiltless while the altar was spoiled.

The Dame.

And yet, further, their nest was consumed by the hallowed fire therefore, and themselves in it.

Sewer.

Madam, the guests on horseback have even now turned in at the head of the avenue.

The Dame.

Make all ready, Wallis, to receive them and their beasts.—No casuist am I, Sir Henry, but a fearful woman. I read in Holy Writ, that when sacred things are put to profane use, the curse descendeth to the third and fourth generation. And my one eaglet, the pride and hope of this desolate nest, hath flown abroad, and will be the mark for many a shaft. May the one that is to fly nearest to his heart—

Spelman.

Nay, Madam, I entreat you—

The Dame.

May it not be feathered and winged from the nest itself, by the iniquity of them that went before—

Spelman.

Yet, hear me—

The Dame.

Who took the acres of Clarewell from their God, to bestow them on their vices!—Enough : I have spoken out what hath long lain deep in my soul. You can understand these things; they who dwell around, do but scoff at such a thought. In sooth, they scoff the loudest whose forefathers have shared most in the like spoils.

SPELMAN.

Scoff as they will—for you seem even then most soothed when I contradict not your forebodings—methinks I could number no less than four families, in this shire only, that have planted themselves in holy ground, and on whom have descended such judgments as are notable, even to all men.

THE DAME.

They feel the rod, yet will not confess the hand that smites.

SPELMAN.

Such mirth must sound on your ear like the Babylonish songs at Balthasar's banquet, while the besotted ones, who were to sink into hell that night, quaffed their drunken guilt out of the consecrated gold and silver from the Temple.

THE DAME.

Look into that slip of paper, folded up amid the parchments. Know you not the hand-writing? it is that of my lord, who had—you wot—a nice and curious taste in rendering verses from the Latin. He lit upon the original lines on his travel in foreign parts; methinks 'twas in the English College of Douay: and being struck therewith—for we shared our fears, as well as our fortunes and brief happiness—

Spelman.

Here is the Latin beside it. Truly, a faithful version; though it be difficult to compress our larger and more rugged tongue within the concinnity of speech used by that Rome, that was once the mother of us all.

The Dame.

But whose mother-tongue we have left, together with so much else belonging thereto. Fear not to read it aloud: for I have it off, like a knell that hath struck repeatedly on the ear of an anxious listener.

Spelman.

" Dear bought; for thou must one day undergo
  The price of this—hell, darkness, fire, and woe;
  God's threats are sure, though mercy be among
    them;
  He guards His rights, and pays them home that
    wrong them!"*

---

* Vos male gaudetis, quia tandem suscipietis
  Nequitiæ fructum, tenebras, incendia, luctum:
  Nam pius indultor, justusque tamen Deus ultor
  Quæ sua sunt munit, quæ sunt hostilia punit.

A translation for which thanks are due to the editors of a late edition of Spelman's *History of Sacrilege*.

The Dame.

Here comes the trampling of your friends' horses. Pray you, excuse me to them with all civility. If I could not encounter them before, less able am I now. Grief hath its privileges, which I claim: meanwhile, this poor house is yours and theirs, so long as it pleaseth you to use it: and so, farewell.

Spelman.

Alack, poor soul! do what I might to put a good face on't, I fear me, she could not but note my thoughts, in my own despite. Aye, true it is—true from the days of Core and his company, even till now. The earth no longer opens, by a miracle that strike the senses, to swallow them up at every turn. What then? By swifter steps than others who journey to the tomb—by stranger and more awful paths, they go under the earth, and are no more seen. "Truly, there is a God that judgeth!"

Sewer.

Honoured Knight, here be arrived Master William Dugdale and one Master Dodsworth, together with a third, whom I know not; but who seemeth, by his garb, a seminarist from beyond seas.

Spelman.

Admit them with reverence, Wallis. I marvel

whom they have brought with them. And in priestly habit? Why, 'tis against the Statute, if he be a seminarist indeed. Perchance, a disciple of Nicolas Ferrar, or some other of that small body of men, more taken with singularities than abundant in sterling sense; who sport before the Church of Rome even as kittens before a mirror, and running round to find the substance of what engaged their curiosity, find the same self they thought to have left on the other side:—ha! mine antient friend, thrice welcome! and you, too, Master Dodsworth. One may see, by your trunk-hose, ye have ridden far through our miry bye-ways.

DUGDALE.

Give welcome also to our companion of the road, whom, journeying partly the same way, we have with difficulty persuaded to share our lodging and entertainment.

SPELMAN.

Honoured, and, as I may suppose, reverend sir, I am your most observant. I pray you, Master Dugdale, by what name am I to know your guest and ours?

DUGDALE.

Truly, in the interest of our discourse by the way, that is the point I have failed to enquire.

Priest.

I am called Diego Alvarez, and, though unworthy, occupy the post of almoner and domestic chaplain to his Excellency, the Ambassador from Spain.

Spelman.

Right welcome, in name of the Lady Cureton. The more so, Don Diego, that being under protection of the Spanish flag, ye voyage among us unquestioned—or, if question arise, not disallowed.

Don Diego.

Worthy sir and host, it seemeth me a strange thing, that being a priest should offer hindrance to a man's pursuing his lawful affairs on one brink of a narrow channel, when it inspireth confidence and putteth him forward on the other.

Spelman.

You say truly, mine honoured guest ; nor are we all in England insensible to the loss we have suffered in breaking from communion with the rest of Christendom. But enough of this: even so are our evil times.

Dugdale.

Let us rather ask what be those antient deeds in your hand?

Spelman.

Even now was I perusing them, and with such feelings as you will share with me. Listen only to the confirmation of the charter by which this poor house and its scanty lands were held : it was given by the Pope of that day, Innocent the Fourth.

Dodsworth.

And how came in its present mouldy state?

Spelman.

It shall be a tale for you when dinner is served: and no common one. In the meanwhile, list ye to the contents, which run thus :

"We therefore decree, that no man whatsoever shall presume to disturb the aforesaid monastery, to take its possessions, nor to retain them when taken, not to diminish the same, nor to put them to wear and tear, nor to molest them in anywise. But let all things be kept whole and sound, so as shall every way profit them, for whose rule and maintenance they were granted; saving the authority of the Apostolic See, and the canonical rights of the diocesan bishops. Wherefore if any person, ecclesiastical or secular, shall hereafter knowingly presume to essay or attempt aught against the letter of this our present Constitution, let him, after the second or third admonition, and except he shall amend his crime by due satisfaction, be deprived of all pre-eminence of power and of honour that were his: and let him know himself to be guilty of the judgment of God for the iniquity he hath committed: and let him be deprived of the most Sacred Body and Blood of God, our Lord and Redeemer, Jesus Christ, and at the last Judgment lie under His vengeance without mercy. Amen—Amen—Amen."

Don Diego.

So was it ever with the head of the Church universal: whose office was, on the one hand, to foster every work of piety and self-denial among the children of that great family, and, on the other, to denounce the judgments of his Master on all such as should hinder or bring them to nought.

Spelman.

We being all here greatly of one mind, I would adventure, not now a reading, but a narration, that bears no little on this same so fearful matter.

Dodsworth.

With all my heart.

Don Diego.

And to attentive ears.

SPELMAN.

Thus, then, it fell out: and you must have the courtesy to believe yourselves for a short space living in the first years of King Henry III.

William Marshall, Earl of Pembroke, the great protector both of king and kingdom, having, in the Irish war, forcibly taken from the Bishop of Ferns two manors belonging to his Church, was by him much solicited to restore them ; but the Earl refusing, was by the Bishop excommunicated, and so dying, was buried in the Temple Church at London. The Bishop sues to the King to return the lands ; the King requires the Bishop to absolve the Earl, and both King and Bishop go to the Earl's grave, where the Bishop, in the King's presence, used these words :

"O William! who liest here snared in the bonds of excommunication, if what thou hast injuriously taken from my Church be with competent satisfaction restored, either by the King, thy heirs, or friend, I then absolve thee ; otherwise I ratify my sentence. *Ut tuis semper peccatis involutus in inferno maneas condemnatus:* that thou mayest ever abide, bound about with thy sins, in the damnation of hell."

DODSWORTH.

Truly, an austere sentence, and such, methinks,

as barely consists with Christian charity. But I would fain know the opinion of our guest; and, on so grave a matter, intreat him to speak freely.

Don Diego.

We have not as yet heard the end of the story; but, so far as it hath proceeded, it is plain to remark the Bishop only acted as an instrument of Him who hath said, "Vengeance is mine: I will repay." He wisheth not the evil—God forbid—he doth but declare it; and with so much greater authority than a preacher who denounceth God's enemies in every sermon, as he hath been by Him exalted to greater authority both of blessing and malediction.

Spelman.

So, I proceed: The King blames the Bishop's rigour, and persuades the sons to a restitution. But the eldest, William, answered: he did not believe his father to have got them unjustly, because possessions got in war become a lawful inheritance. "And, therefore, if the doting old Bishop hath judged falsely, upon his own head be the curse. My father died seised of them, and I lawfully inherit them, nor will I lessen my estate."

Which the Bishop hearing, was more grieved at the son's contumacy than at the father's injustice, and going to the King, said to him:

"Sir, what I have said stands immutable: the punishment of malefactors is from the Lord. And the curse written in the Psalms will fall heavy upon Earl William. In the next generation shall his name be forgot; his sons shall not share that blessing, 'Increase and multiply;' and some of them shall die miserable deaths, and the inheritance of all be dispersed and scattered. And all this, my lord, O King, you shall see even in your days."

Don Diego.

See you? 'tis even as I said: he doth but declare that over which he hath no control. But prythee, proceed.

Spelman.

With what spirit, or prescience of the future, perhaps beyond his own powers of forecasting, the Bishop spoke it, do ye judge; for, in the space of twenty-five years, all the five sons of the Earl successively, according to their birth, inherit his earldom and lands, and all die childless. The name and family became extinct, and the lands scattered and dispersed; and, that nothing might fail of what the Bishop foretold, Richard, the second son, is sore wounded and taken prisoner in Ireland, and there dies of his hurt; Gilbert, the third son, jousting at Hertford, breaks the reins of his bridle, and falling from his horse, one foot hangs in the stirrup, and he thereby dragged about the field, till rent and torn, and so by a miserable death satisfied the curse.*

DODSWORTH.

I see not here any miraculous powers of prophecy.

DUGDALE.

Nor I; but rather judge that the Bishop drew from general principles, and belike from observation, such conclusion as we can see yet more clearly who look up the stream of time.

DODSWORTH.

Hear what is said, not by a Bishop, but by one of our antient Saxon kings, on this very matter of spoliation. "It is an horrible thing," saith he,† "for men to rob the living God, and to divide His portion and raiment among themselves."

DUGDALE.

Ah, that all kings had been affected by so true a

---

* This story, with much of the context, is taken word for word from Spelman's *English Works*, pref. p. xvii., as quoted from Matthew Paris, fol. 687. Speed, p. 579, ed. 1632, mentions the death of "the great Marshal, Earl of Pembroke," in 1219, and his five sons successively inheriting and dying childless; but without assigning any reason.

† King Wihtred, in the Council of Beccancelde.

sense of its horribleness! I well believe, the troubles that seem in store for our country would have been spared us. King and subjects would understand one another better at this day, had they not all drank so deep of that cup of guilt.

DODSWORTH.

Will future times ever believe the vast amount of treasure, once dedicated to God's altar, that was poured through the sieve of the Royal purse an hundred years since, and nothing retained but the sin, and the curse that clave to it?

DON DIEGO.

Tell me, sir, I pray you: for I know not the particulars.

DODSWORTH.

Nay, then, the revenue that came to King Henry VIII. in ten years was more than four times that of the Crown lands, besides an untold heap of treasure raised out of the money, jewels, plate, ornaments, and implements of churches, monasteries, and religious houses, with their farms and granges, goods and cattle. At his first dissolution, of the smaller houses, three hundred seventy and five abodes of prayer and charity were swept away; again, less than four years after, six hundred forty and six of the larger sort. Ninety-six colleges, not in the Universities, one hundred and ten hospitals, two thousand three hundred seventy and four chantries and free chapels, with about seven hundred Irish monasteries added thereto.

Don Diego.

Can this be indeed true, my honoured friend? As you speak, it sounds like a voice from the other world. It is as a muttering of inexorable vengeance for such unheard-of spoliation.

Spelman.

And, even in this world, what was the end? Spite of the vast sums which that king inherited from his father, and the boundless wealth (as I may say) that came into his coffers on the fall of Wolsey, together with the spoils just now rehearsed, yet was he so reduced to poverty that, to build a few blockhouses for defence of the coast, he had recourse, the very next year, to a fresh subsidy, beside the many former extortions, of four-fifteenths from his subjects; and afterwards was brought so low as to debase the coinage of the realm, and even to stamp leather money.*

* See Camden's *Britannia*, fol. 163.

DUGDALE.

True is it, poverty came both to crown and country by that same sacrilege. While our religious houses stood, they employing their revenues according to the direction of the founders of each several house, and the spirit of them all in common, opened wide their hospitable gates to all comers, and without the charges of a reckoning, welcomed all travellers alike, without such proud distinctions as the Apostle Saint James reproveth: so that rich and poor, noble and serf, ate under the same roof, after having prayed before the same altar.

Thus did they relieve all the neighbouring poor, without bringing in any warrant from the two nighest Justices of the Peace, nor curse of penal law.

DODSWORTH.

While those walls stood, or, rather, were tenanted by them for whom they were builded, the younger children, both of lords and commons, were provided for, without the ruin of their fathers' estate, and not left (as now) often to an unworthy, necessitous, and vicious course of life.

SPELMAN.

We had then no new laws, the offspring of new vices, to compel us to erect houses of correction for vicious and vagrant persons, to provide stock to bind poor children 'prentices, nor to make constant levies to maintain the weak, lame, indigent, and persons enfeebled by age; nor that annual subsidy —or yet more often—that hath now come in as a custom from the necessity of these evil times.

Don Diego.

I have heard so much within this half hour that is familiar to my own thoughts, methinks it is strange, mine honoured host and friends, ye pursue not these principles to their full conclusion. But, that I may contribute somewhat to your discourse, listen to the form of dedication of religious houses and lands in use in the time of Charlemagne, as we learn from his capitular.

Dugdale.

I doubt not, 'tis as solemn, neither more nor less, as those in use among our own forefathers.

Don Diego.

Thus it ran. The founder, mentioning in a writing all he intended to give, and holding it over the altar, spoke thus to the priest: " I here give unto God all things contained in this writing, for the remission of my sins, &c., and for them for whose benefit God may will to accept them: and by these to promote God's service by the holy Sacrifice, by lights (for the altar, &c.), by support of the clergy, the poor, and in all things that are to the glory of God and benefit of His Church; and if any man shall take these away (which God forbid!) let him, for his sacrilege, give a most strict account to God, to whom they are now dedicated and devoted"—and so it runs on, in a like strain.

Dodsworth.

Truly, the principle is one so plain, it "jumps," as they say in France, "to one's eyes." If all history were silent, and barren of any example, of the fate which spoilers have undergone, yet might we reason on it, with the schoolmen, *à priori*, and come out to the same conclusion.

Don Diego.

Yet one thing strikes me, now we speak of reasoning, were I but sure of uttering it without shadow of offence.

Spelman.

Of that be well assured, in the name of all the company.

Don Diego.

Ye speak, then, worthy sirs, of spoiling God's altar for the gold thereof: but had there been none other sacrilege, I pray you, done in England before it, and did none follow after? What of all the changes in religion whereby those altars were not only stripped but pulled down, and Genevan tables set in the chancels? what of abolishing the daily Sacrifice, and setting the Royal Supremacy, like an "abomination that maketh desolate," in the holy place? Methinks, the prophet Dániel would have told you, your lament over the sin and fate of sacrilege was altogether partial and one-sided. "For whether is greater, the gold, or the altar that sanctifieth the Gold?" What shall I say of this very house, that was ever a poor Franciscan friary, yet from which the rood was torn down, the altar-tapers quenched, the brethren expelled, and—

Sewer.

Honoured sirs, your poor repast awaits you.

PREFACE TO AGE THE SIXTH.

Yet ruder, coarser lineaments are now
Shown, half reluctant, on the changeful page:
Low hath it sunk, the fane despoil'd; more low
Sinks in dark ruin, through degenerate age.
Forms all incongruous haunt what once was fair,
Now faith is fled, and whatso raiseth man:
A den of thieves is grown that house of prayer,
Time's Proteus-play reveals them to our scan.
Harsh, yet historic scene: as when the light
Casts on some camera's lens a truthful ray;
While each ungainly line stands forth to sight,
We fain would soften, may not hide away!
Enough is here to show what days are gone:
Our task fulfill'd, thankful we speed us on.

The Seven Ages of Claretwell.

AGE THE SIXTH: 1736.

DESECRATED.

(THE KITCHEN, PARTLY UNROOFED AND RUINOUS).

FIRST COINER.

Now, let's begin.

SECOND COINER.

Not yet: Hugh is out, scouting round; the game-keeper might be coming this way with his helpers.

THIRD COINER.

'Tis a dark night, and a wild one; don't much think he'll trouble us. I'll go and fish out the melting pot, where I hid it at day-break, in the bushes.

SECOND COINER.

Don't know: he's got an odd fashion of popping

on a man unawares. Remember last winter, when poor Tom—

OWL.

Tu-whit! tu-whoo-hu-hoo-oo-oo!

FIRST COINER.

Well, man, we've our pistols too, and other pretty tools. Catch a gentleman of the Mint without his pistols! we're able to entertain half a dozen keepers.

THIRD COINER.

And reason good, if we're molested in our calling. Why, even in the London banking-houses, they've a blunderbuss and a brace of horse-pistols hanging within reach of the cashier.

FIRST COINER.

What do *you* know, Jones, about London banking-houses, I should like to know?

THIRD COINER.

Wasn't I employed on the building of the Bank of England, that was opened three years ago? I know every stone of the place, and could get into it from Lothbury, with a little assistance.

SECOND COINER.

Some of our productions, at least, have seen the inside of their strong rooms.

THIRD COINER.

Got mixed with the others. Aye, if sovereigns could speak, and tell their stories, there'd be a pretty account of their adventures.

OWL.

Tu-whit! tu-whoo-hu-hoo-oo-oo!

SECOND COINER.

And the most amusing would be, the history of a *bad* sovereign.

FIRST COINER.

D'ye mean, a bad king? for we are pretty well supplied in that way, just now.

SECOND COINER.

Aye, Jem, we know you of old for a cantankerous Jacobite. Take care, lad, 'tis almost as bad as coining.

FIRST COINER.

Worse, by a good deal. If you're a coiner, when they catch you, they hang you. But if you're an honest man, they draw you on a hurdle from Newgate up the Oxford Road, with your head knickety-knocking, string you up, cut you down alive—

SECOND AND THIRD COINERS.

Honest man!

BAT.

Tri-tri-tri!

THIRD COINER.

Speak for yourself! Why isn't a coiner an honest man?

FIRST COINER.

You know what I mean, by this time o' day. A coiner's a right honest fellow; for he does what your London banker does—supply folks with money—

THIRD COINER.

Aye, now: that's something like.

OWL.

Tu-whit! tu whoo-hu-hoo-oo-oo!

FIRST COINER.

But I don't call that man honest, who truckles to such a government as—

SECOND COINER.

Right enough: no governments. Every government has its officers: and they are a kind of folks that I—

GIPSY HORSE DEALER.

All friends! I thought I'd drop in, on the chance of finding some of you here, in the old place.

Second Coiner.

And at the old trade.

Gipsy.

The place is older than the trade, I take it.

Third Coiner.

Not a whit, man: some of those lordly abbots of antient days had the privilege of the Mint, and issued their own coins.

Fourth Coiner.

Aye? so this old cloister has known the clink of the coiner's hammer, before now?

Second Coiner.

Not such a house as this: a poor friary, that can hardly have been worth the trouble of harrying. Hallo, there's Hugh's whistle. Come in, lad.

Fourth Coiner.

All safe and snug, so far as I could see. Not a sound stirring, only the deer rubbing their antlers against the trees. Not so much as a squirrel snoring.

Bat.

Tri-tri-tri!

Second Coiner.

Up with us, then, and begin.

First Coiner.

All I say is; no man here can tell whether, five years hence, he may be stamping King George's head, or King James'. A sovereign's a sovereign: but I'd rather have the right head on mine. I've a qualm of conscience, every Guelph I strike off for circulation.

Third Coiner.

Five years, man! why, we may be hanging in chains, long before then. Get the charcoal out of that nook in the old chapel, and let's begin.

Owl.

Tu-whit! tu-whoo-hu-hoo-oo-oo!

Fourth Coiner.

Hsh! a step—

First Coiner.

Ay? look to your priming, lads.

First Pistol.

Click!

Second Pistol.

Click, click!

AGE THE SIXTH—DESECRATED.

PRIEST (in disguise).

A friend!

SECOND COINER.

Friend? what sort of a one, though?

THIRD COINER.

One of the Society of Friends, belike? They're grave-looking folks, too.

PRIEST.

Hold down your weapons. I, at least, do not betray you. I am in danger myself.

THIRD COINER.

And how may that be?

SECOND COINER.

Who are after you—for what?

PRIEST.

For my blood, and for money.

FOURTH COINER.

Aye, money buys blood, all the world over. But what are you in for?

THIRD COINER.

Or out for?

Priest.

It would take long to explain. Besides, no one is bound to accuse himself.

Second Coiner.

Right enough: only, there are some gentry we should'nt like to house with. You can take pot-luck with us, if you prove to be none of them.

Priest.

Aye? will you furnish me with a list?

Third Coiner.

Well, now: nothing of murder, or knocking people on the head?

Second Coiner.

Except in lawful self defence—

Bat.

Tri-tri-tri!

Fourth Coiner.

As we might ha' done to you, had you'd been the gamekeeper.

Second Coiner.

Or the sheriff's officer.

Third Coiner.

Or any one else, unlawfully disturbing our occupation.

Priest.

It is for no crime whatever, great or small.

Third Coiner.

Nor meddling with the house of Brunswick, and the glorious and happy succession of George Guelph, as the man standing at your elbow would, if he could?

Priest.

Whatever my opinions, it is not for anything in that direction.

Second Coiner.

Well, highway robbery, without murder—or forgery, which is a less laborious exercise of our own profession—the higher walk of it, as one may say? or—

Owl.

Tu-whit! tu-whoo-hu-hoo-oo-oo!

Priest.

Spare yourself the trouble: you need not go through the Statute-book. I will trust myself to you.

Third Coiner.

You may. We are not the men to walk into the next town, and lodge an information. We only want to know whether you're respectable.

Priest.

Here is a paper I have about me. It may tell you something.

Fourth Coiner.

Why, it's all in some strange lingo I can't make out. Yet you don't seem a foreigner. You speak English almost as well as us. What does that mean?

Third Coiner.

Let me look. Latin! we'll have none of it, except to conjure by. Hark ye, stranger, can you transmute the metals, belike? Art master of the philosopher's stone? We'll hail you one of ourselves.

Fourth Coiner.

These old walls have seen such doings in their day, I've heard. There was one Friar Bacon, now, who practised amazingly, by all accounts. Why, he made a brazen head, that could tell—

PRIEST.

My friends, it may not matter to you much to know who or what I am, further than this: I am no spy, no informer, no one whom any just or upright laws would persecute. Yet, like yourselves, I am under the edge of the law at this moment.

SECOND COINER.

Why, now, that's sensible talk.

THIRD COINER.

Of course, if laws are bad, they persecute honest men.

FOURTH COINER.

The very thing you may read on that board over the park-paling, a stone's throw from this: "Whosoever trespasses in these grounds will be persecuted according to law." There's laws for you!

PRIEST.

If we followed out all that much further, we might soon differ—

THIRD COINER.

Differ? then we'd best do it at once, and know who you are.

OWL.

Tu-whit! tu-whoo-hu-hoo-oo-oo!

PRIEST.

So, I come back to what I said. An unjust law, through no fault of mine, compels me to hide my head. This is why you see me here.

THIRD COINER.

Aye; and so an unjust law made bold Robin Hood take to the good green wood, and range with his merry men all of a row, through the forest in which this old place was built.

FOURTH COINER.

And an unjust law made me give my creditors the slip, when the South Sea bubble burst, and lead a wandering life, to escape a jail-fever in the Fleet.

SECOND COINER.

And made me break my parish indentures, and take to the King's highway.

PRIEST.

That hardly passes, my friend. No law, however harsh, can drive a man to what is wrong.

SECOND COINER.

So? then we are at sixes and sevens again, instead of on the square.

BAT.

Tri-tri-tri!

AGE THE SIXTH—DESECRATED.

THIRD COINER.

Wrong, quotha? who says I did wrong to come here, and increase the wealth of the nation?

SECOND COINER.

And help many an honest man to a loaf of bread?

FOURTH COINER.

And pay his rent?

THIRD COINER.

Didn't you say, yourself, you were under the edge of the law?

PRIEST.

True: but I do no wrong to incur it.

FOURTH COINER.

What are you, after all? knock his hat off, Bill.

PRIEST.

I will save you the trouble. I've no concealment from you: though it would be enough to say, I am in danger, and in hiding, by no fault of my own; and I claim a morsel of food, and a corner for the night.

THIRD COINER.

What made you come here?

PRIEST.

It was the most natural place for me to come to.

SECOND COINER.

Natural? by what right?

OWL.

Tu-whit! tu-whoo-hu-hoo-oo-oo!

PRIEST.

Well, friends, if we come to *right*, I've a better right to find shelter here than most men in England.

FOURTH COINER.

Hark in your ear, Jones; what if this be one of the family, come back to claim his own? the heir was beyond seas—he may be here, with his followers waiting outside.

SECOND COINER.

True enough. Hallo, lads, look sharp!

FIRST PISTOL.

Click! click!

THIRD COINER.

What, barkers again? nay, then—

Second Pistol.

Click! click!

First Coiner.

No harm in being ready, so—

Third Pistol.

Click! click!

Third Coiner.

What's all this about, stranger?

Priest.

That's what I was going to ask. What have I said to make you suspect me again?

Second Coiner.

That you'd a right to be here.

Third Coiner.

Now, if you have, we haven't, that's clear. But we have, if might be right; why then, you haven't: so move off—

Fourth Coiner.

Quick—

Third Coiner.

Or else—

PRIEST.

If I shew you, my right is one I cannot claim, and am not come even to beg for, beyond the shelter of to-night?—

SECOND COINER.

Why, that's another matter again: eh, lads?

OWL.

Tu-whit! tu-whoo-hu-hoo-oo-oo!

PRIEST.

And if my right has not been exercised, or claimed, for two hundred years—

THIRD COINER.

Hallo! what romancing is this, now?

FOURTH COINER.

Two hundred years? and yet you stand up there before us?

SECOND COINER.

Two hundred years? aha, I smell a rat. Now, deal with us on the square. You're a Roman?

PRIEST.

If you like it so: I am a Catholic.

FOURTH COINER.

And a priest?

PRIEST.

Would I were worthy.

THIRD COINER.

Which means yes, I suppose. Does that give you a right to be here?

PRIEST.

Why, who built this place, and for whom?

FOURTH COINER.

And who took the roof off, and beat down the Cross? Come, I think I matched you there.

PRIEST.

You ought to have added, for whom? my friend. Then both questions would have been complete.

SECOND COINER.

Make it so: and answer both.

PRIEST.

I will. Who built this place? Catholics who had this world's substance, and wished to spend it for the glory of their Maker, and good of their souls.

For whom did they build it? For a community of friars, who should chant psalms of praise in their choir, preach to the people in their nave, study and write out useful books in their library, and relieve the poor with daily alms and food at their gate.

Second Coiner.

Well, that's pat enough, so far. Now for the other question. You've earned half your shake-down and supper: may be the second half will follow.

Priest.

Who ruined it? an impious king, who valued no more the lives and property of his subjects than I should scruple to lift my staff and behead yon foxglove on the wall.

For whom? For himself, that he might fill his coffers, exhausted by his personal luxury and extravagance; and for his profligate courtiers, who would win or lose a religious house by a bet on hawk or hound, or a cast of the dice.

Third Coiner.

What is to be thought of all this?

First Coiner.

Thought? that it's true, every word of it.

AGE THE SIXTH—DESECRATED. 167

OWL.

Tu-whit! tu-whoo-hu-hoo-oo-oo!

FOURTH COINER.

Aha, Jem: so you, too, are Roman as well as Jacobite?

FIRST COINER.

No one put me through my catechism, when I put my neck into a halter to join you.

GIPSY.

Right enough, lad: the first and last question is at the Assise.

PRIEST.

Not quite that, friends: "after death, the Judgment."

THIRD COINER.

Enough said. You'll swear not to betray us?

PRIEST.

I have nothing against taking any lawful oath, though I am accustomed to have my word believed.

FOURTH COINER.

You're a kind of a Chinese puzzle, that's the truth.

Fourth Coiner.

Aye, all this is French to me. But we've battered the point enough, and we might have melted an ingot by this time. Come, lads, look sharp.

Third Coiner.

Fetch you the charcoal, Robin.

Priest.

Nay, then, I leave you.

Fourth Coiner.

Wind's chopped round again?

Priest.

Not so; I am weary to an extremity, and to go forth again in this wild night is as much as my life is worth.

Gipsy.

When you're allowed to stay, then, I advise you to stay. Never throw away a chance.

Priest.

I cannot remain and witness what is unlawful.

Owl.

Tu-whit! tu-whoo-hu-hoo-oo-oo!

Second Coiner.

And you can't expect us to change our way of life, because it don't happen to jump with your likings.

Smuggler, *outside.*

Who's for himself?

Second Coiner.

Aye, that's a safe watch-word: shall I give the countersign? It's all right, I learned it on the Suffolk coast.

Third Coiner.

Ay, ay.

Second Coiner.

A man of sense.

Smuggler.

All right, I find. Good evening gentlemen. Well, I've heard this old tumble-down place lay not far from my line of march to some inland customers. But I'm not a tourist, d'y see: don't go about making sketches of ruins and castles; so I've never been here before.

Fourth Coiner.

'Tis enough for us, if the vaults, and so forth, of

such ruins, are as weather-tight as could well be expected.

Smuggler.

I've had a smart run for it;—two mounted gaugers sighted me, and this small keg, on the hill. It was all I could do to gain the wood; as I lay panting in the ditch, I heard them slashing the bushes with their cutlasses within arm's length of me. At last I slunk off, like a hare when the hounds puzzle about the scent: afraid to snap a stick, or crackle a leaf, to betray me.

Second Coiner.

Then they'll be coming this way: we'd best be ready.

Smuggler.

No fear—the place, you know, has a character for being haunted. Many a stout fellow, now, would face anything you might name, as long as daylight lasted, who wouldn't be over fond of finding himself within half a mile of these ruins after night-fall.

Gipsy.

Aye, indeed?—and why might that be?

Third Coiner.

Nay, you Egyptians, or Bohemians, are supposed

to deal in the black arts yourselves, and don't mind such things, I suppose. I don't care who hears me say it: I'd rather find myself here in merry company, than alone.

OWL.

Tu-whit! tu-whoo-hu-hoo-oo-oo!

GIPSY.

But why these ruins, more than any others?

SMUGGLER.

Hardly know: you wouldn't feel comfortable, now, to find yourself at night under a gibbet, when the wind sways the creaking irons and the rattling bones to and fro?

GIPSY.

That's a different thing. I've felt it, not many days back. As the bones rattle, they seem to go on chattering, chattering:

To-day for me:
To-morrow for thee!

till one's teeth begin to chatter for company.

SMUGGLER.

Well; the difference?

GIPSY.

The gibbet was put up for—for—

COINERS.

Oh, don't be nice: speak out!

GIPSY.

Well, for gentlemen who may swing there yet: but this place was built for monks. Now, there's no danger of my being a monk: so I feel quite easy here.

SMUGGLER.

Here's a grave man in the corner who listens to all, and says nothing. Who is he? what say you, friend, is the place haunted?

PRIEST.

First tell me; what is meant by a place being haunted?

OWL.

Swoop!—Tu-whit! tu-hoo-oo-oo!

ALL, but PRIEST and GIPSY.

What's that?—what's that!—

GIPSY.

Ha, ha! a brave set of fellows! why, a silly, harmless owl!

SECOND COINER.

It lives up in the ruins of yon tower.

AGE THE SIXTH—DESECRATED. 173

THIRD COINER.

Aye, its been sailing in and out through the windows, half the night: but—I don't know what made it come so close just then!

PRIEST.

By a haunted place, then, you mean a place visited by an owl?

SECOND COINER.

Not so, but revisited by ghosts.

FIRST COINER.

Come, you needn't say the word: country folks say "good people," when they mean those who might be offended if you called them fairies; and so—

OWL.

Swoop!—Tu-whit! tu-hoo-oo-oo!

THIRD COINER.

There, again! Enough of all this, I say—it's getting to a point I don't like.

PRIEST.

I believe the place *is* haunted: for there is no ghost like an uneasy conscience.

Sucond Coiner.

'Tis long since I have heard that word: but a truce to the whole business. Come, the melting pot, I say.

Third Coiner.

Aye, aye:—blow up the fire, and show a cheerful light.

Priest.

Then I go. Farewell, my friends; may better thoughts than you seem to know at present bring you to some other and safer line of life.

First Coiner.

I don't like to see you leave us. If you *will* go, let me see you safe out of the wood.

Fourth Coiner.

Hallo! who sneaks off?

First Coiner.

Not I, for one.

Priest.

I should be glad, indeed, to take you with me: and so would you, when life is over.

Third Coiner.

Aye, but it isn't over yet. Remember our articles

First Coiner.

I go as far as the edge of the wood, to put this stranger on his way.

Smuggler.

To put him into the hands of the gaugers? they are ferreting about still, I'll lay any money.

Priest.

I have no way. There is a warrant out against me for saying Mass: whithersoever I turn, my path is equally unsafe. I leave you, because your occupation is unlawful: but the wood must be my shelter, or the moor my path, to-night.

Third Coiner.

Not our fault. We offered you such lodging as we have.

Priest.

The day will come—I cannot doubt it—when these ruined walls will be given back to the use for which their founder built them. You and I will have long passed away, before then: each to our account—to our doom. My time is very near: yours will not be far. Repent, while the hour is yours, for to-morrow may give you to that Enemy, out of whose clutch is no redemption. Farewell.

The Seven Ages of Clarewell.

AGE THE SEVENTH: 1836.

RESTORED.

(THE RUINED CHOIR AND REFECTORY, SEPARATED BY BROKEN WALLS AND ONE SIDE OF CLOISTER, ALMOST WITHIN EAR-SHOT ONE OF THE OTHER).

HARRY (coming into the Choir).

Why, George! we lost you: I have hunted the ruins for you, high and low! nearly broke my neck through the window of the infirmary, I fancy, or sick abbot's dormitory, or something. An infirmary case, that would have been, eh? with no Friar Bacon to attend me: they say, he was no mean doctor, for his day.—Dreaming still, man? Dost perpetrate a ballad, or art thou studying the architecture of this old place?

GEORGE.

To say truth, Harry, the place *does* put me into a brown study.

Harry.

Brown? to judge from your rueful visage, very dark brown: and that, with the sunlight through those mullions, glinting on the ivy, and merry birds chirping in and out!

George.

Even so: even therefore. What a contrast between this life of nature, vigorous and cheery, with motion, energy, enjoyment, yet partly unconscious, little suggestive—and, on the other hand—

Harry.

Nay, can't wait for the other hand. You'll join us, though?

George.

Immediately; pray make yourselves at home. Tell my servant to unpack the hamper, and bring the case of champagne into the old refectory, since you are bent on it. A fitter place for luncheon could hardly be, you'll allow.

Harry.

Come, I'm glad to see you smile; *salva res est*. I thought you were conversing with the ghost of a defunct abbot; on the point of pronouncing your vows, or resigning the estate again into his hands.

George.

Abbot? this was a Franciscan friary.

Harry.

Friar; I humbly beg his pardon: sorry we can't offer him a glass of champagne. If all tales are true, the jolly monks of old would hardly decline such a toll from us, for intruding on their precincts.

George.

Aye, Harry, if all tales were true; which they are not.

Harry.

You don't believe in the jollity of the reverend fathers?

George.

In their happiness, and cheerfulness, I believe— so far as they were faithful to their vocation.

Harry.

Psha! you know what I mean—that they liked their glass as well as you or I? nay, excluding you, as I and Walter, and the rest.

George.

Naturally, I dare say, they would have sung, like you and Walter,

> *Huc vinum, et unguenta, et nimium breves*
> *Flores amœnæ ferre jube rosæ :—*

and so to the end. They were *men*, even as the Apostles said to those to whom they preached. Had they not been, they would not have retired hither for their own sakes, nor preached to the neighbouring peasants with much good result.— But—

HARRY.

But?

GEORGE.

Well, I suppose what you think about them may be one of the many things that are true, and not true.

HARRY.

True and not true? A Delphic oracle. "Declare thyself less darkly."

GEORGE.

I mean; true here, untrue there: true in the case of A. B., but untrue and calumnious in that of C. D.; untrue, point-blank, in times of fervour; lamentably true—"be the same more or less"—in times of relaxation and deadness. That's my paraphrase.

HARRY.

Hm.

GEORGE.

You remember, the preamble of the Act of Henry VIII. for suppressing the smaller monasteries, three centuries back—by the bye, this very year, three hundred years ago—acknowledges, inconsistently enough, the good discipline of the larger ones—

HARRY.

Says Yes or No, I dare say, just as the humour of that ferocious old tyrant dictated at the moment. Nevertheless, you have made a considerable abatement to your But.

GEORGE.

My But remains; for—

HARRY.

Pop! there goes the first bottle of champagne. Come, man: here's a Horace for your Horace;

Sapias, vina liques, et spatio brevi
Spem longam reseces: dum loquimur, fugerit invida
Ætas, carpe diem—

Still in a trance? *au revoir*, then: Gilbert has promised us his best song. We'll keep a nook of the pasty for you, and a fag-end of the Epernay.

ANGEL.

Hath not the spirit of this antient place
Enter'd within thy heart? the walls that stand
Roofless, denote they not more hallowed days
When man his Maker serv'd, himself subdued?

Breathes there no voice, the vacant cloister through,
Mourning those ten full ages desolate
Since the proud spoiler's hand great Heaven defied,
Tore down God's altar, quell'd the voice of prayer?

GEORGE.

How deep a sense appears to possess me, at this moment, of what these ruins once were, and what they have so long become! I've been here, again and again, musing, dreaming among them: yet never felt it so strongly—

GILBERT (from the Refectory).

The monk must arise when the matins ring,
The abbot may sleep to their chime;—

GEORGE.

I have often tried to re-construct, in fancy, the old materials out of these ruinous heaps, and build them up in their shapeliness once more—

GILBERT.

But the yeoman must start when the bugles sing,
'Tis time, my hearts! 'tis time!

GEORGE.

I have repeopled the empty cloister, until the friar's grey frock has seemed to glide before me in the deepening twilight. But this is a new thought; comes, at least, with a new power.

GILBERT.

But the yeoman must start when the bugles sing:—

GEORGE.

Is it fancy, or is it faith? I am no poet, nor ever was: so far, unworthy to have inherited a spot so beautiful, even in its ruins; and yet—

GILBERT.

'Tis time, my hearts! 'tis time!

GEORGE.

But ought I to inherit it at all? that is the first question, and no light one—

GILBERT.

Here, Walter, quick! Harry, your glass! "Swift wine," Homer says, doesn't he?

GEORGE.

It was not built for me, or mine; nor for any use we can put it to. They tried that for an hundred and twenty years, after the dissolution: and see what came of it:—

GILBERT.

The abbot may sleep to their chime;

George.

Family misfortunes, attainders, beheadings—

Walter.

And the master of the feast—our Amphitryon? what's become of him?

George.

Sudden, violent deaths—incurable sickness—a slanting inheritance, never descending in a straight line, no, not from that day to this—

Harry.

Oh, you needn't expect him yet: he's dreaming in the choir, yonder. Hark, in your ear, now; I'll tell you a curious thing. Since he's been in possession of the estate—full six months—they say, he's been moping about these ruins more than anything else. The old lady is getting quite anxious about him. Besides his being her eldest surviving son, you know—

Claude.

He's also the purveyor of some first-rate champagne.

Harry.

True, your glass! *glglglug*—I was only going to say, the broad acres came into the family through her. That's another curious thing, by the way: this place has never gone from father to son. Isn't it odd?

GEORGE.

"A something ails it now; the place is curst." Aye, there were maledictions pronounced: and they cleave.

HARRY.

The county history, even, remarks it. I don't think George himself is superstitious on the point; though I know others of the family who had just as soon it hadn't been Church-land, and don't much like to hear it talked about—

GILBERT.

Neither do I like to hear about anything so dry. Why, man, you might be the family solicitor. Don't inflict on us the old parchments, and musty deeds. Who's for a song?

GEORGE.

For three hundred years, no prayer has risen up from this sanctuary! A deadly blank, that, in the history of this great prayerless and loveless world. It is like a face with an eye taken out of it. Three hundred years, out of eighteen? why, that is the sixth of Christianity.

WALTER.

Another slice of that ham—thanks.

GEORGE.

I'll step this way: aye, here I stand, just where a friar's *miserere** once stood against the choir-wall. No, let me go down lower, westward. Probably, hereabouts was the Warden's stall: the Sub-Warden there, opposite, both facing the altar—

GILBERT.

I'll give thee, good fellow, a twelvemonth or twain,
To search Europe through, from Byzantium to Spain:

GEORGE.

From this spot, with all his brethren around him, three long hundred years ago, and then for the last time, the Warden of Clarewell looked towards the altar, as it stood under that faultless east window.

GILBERT.

But ne'er shall you find, though you search till you tire,
So joyous a soul as the bare-footed friar!

* In the old monastic and cathedral choirs, the stalls were so constructed, as to afford sufficient support to a person leaning against them nearly upright, to diminish the fatigue of chanting the long night-office in choir.

George.

There is a kind of severe beauty in the simple tracery: aye, one could see, the Franciscans were vowed to poverty, and that of the strictest; and, moreover, that they kept up to it. A two-fold robbery of the poor, this desecration!

Claude.

How does it run? I haven't got the air:

The monk must arise when the matins ring,
　The abbot may sleep—

No; that's not it.

George.

If there was any stained glass at all, it must have been of that pale and merely outlined character that always takes me so much—

Claude.

Aye, so:

But the yeoman must start when the bugles sing—

Gilbert.

Can't compliment you on your success. Try this encouragement: *glugluglug!*

George.

A kind of severe sweetness, and an effort of ideal

art, subdued, consecrated to religion, suggesting more than it expresses: a mortified look, unless I utterly dream, as far above more life-like realism as Francia is above Rubens—

GILBERT.

The friar has walk'd out, and, where'er he has gone,
The land and its fatness is mark'd for his own:—

GEORGE.

Between where I stand, and the foot-pace below the altar, room for how many brethren on a side?

GILBERT (louder).

He can roam where he lists, he can stop when he tires,
For every man's house is the bare-footed friar's!

GEORGE.

There he goes, mad wag! as if he was at an inn! And shame on Walter Scott, to help him to such words—a vile travestie of the truth, as I hope and believe. But such has been the tradition of three centuries—*odisse quem læseris:*—throw plenty of mud, some will stick.

GILBERT.

He can roam where he lists, he can stop when he
  tires—

Demon.

Ho! ho! I've been tortur'd
Oft, by sounds in these walls:
Their vespers, their Sanct-bell,
All through midnight, the drawls
Of those friars! I'd have strangled—
Had I licence—I'd have mangled,
   Chok'd, the shavelings in their stalls!
   Ho, ho, ho!

But that stave *he* trolls there
Glibly chimes with my work:
'Tis bait, while the barbel
Eyes your hook—then, a jerk!
And the fish is all your own—ha!
Tho' he'd lower down his tone—-ha!
   Could he see me, where I lurk—
   Ho, ho, ho!

Walter.

A soldier's a man—a life's but a span—

Claude.

So brim it well up—the monk's wassail cup—

Harry.

That's not in the original.

CLAUDE.

It's germane to the moment, though, and the spot.

DEMON.

Swift I flit between,
Present, while unseen:
Medium none of grosser air
  Makes me here, or there:
    Light nor dark
  Aids, obscures, my mark!
Mine's no dim perception
Drawn from mortal senses;
Almost I can read a mind within,
  I can scent a coming sin
Beyond these earth-worms' best conception:
  My clutching grasp
  A struggling soul can clasp
When I have parried its defences!

CHAMPAGNE BOTTLE.

Pop! fz-z-z-z-glugluglugluglug!

DEMON.

Let well alone:—so best—
Scarcely could safer be:
Quite on another tack
I'll try this dreamer now!

Angel.

Dark spirit, hence! I wave my sword, and lo,
Its brightness, all but visibly reveal'd,
Flashes quick thoughts of good within his brain—

George.

Heavens! what a blessed existence must have been theirs, if they kept up to the mark? Who shall say, they did not? many of them did, I'll lay my life. It was the interest of the most corrupt of Courts to represent them as vile enough to justify the wholesale spoliation :—

Harry.

Seize the moments, while they stay—ay—ay!

George.

A king, the monster idol of an obsequious parliament, threatening to take off some of their heads, if they did not pass his Bill; rapacious courtiers, eager to swoop on their prey—

Harry.

Seize, and use 'em,
Lest you lose 'em—

George.

The royal coffers, exhausted by selfish wars, and selfish luxury, gaping to be filled :—

HARRY.

Lest you lose 'em—

GEORGE.

Cromwell—aye, who will write us a veritable history of those two Cromwells: Thomas first, then Oliver—the representative men of two bad periods?

HARRY.

Seize and use 'em!

GEORGE.

But indeed, as one looks down the stream of history, what period is there that is not chiefly, or merely, the squandering of precious talents—the irreparable loss of golden opportunities?

HARRY.

And lament the wasted day—ay—ay!

DEMON (at his ear).

So your favourite sages say—ay—ay!
Ho, ho, ho!

HARRY.

What's the matter with the wine, all of a sudden?

WALTER.

Well, there *is* something—pah! the mouldering ruins, perhaps, or this old knotted ivy.

Demon.

Nay; we'll crown ourselves with flowers,
   While life runs by!
Noiseless tread the lightsome hours;
   And, if a sigh
From the full heart shall break, 'tis only
That bliss is self, so bliss is lonely,
   With a centering solitude
     Inward, on its chosen good!

Gilbert.

The wine's superb, man:—sulphur? no more than in the *lachrymæ* that grows on Vesuvius. Another bottle, and then we go in search of George, and drag him from his dreams.

Demon.

Not such babblers o'er their drink,
   Sinning in broad day,
     Baulk my ken!
There's a closer race of men
   Who brood, who think
More than they ever say:—
   Yet, even then,
By dint of patience, look on look,
   Comparing, guessing,
    I finish by possessing
A somewhat, like a half-shut book:

As, here a letter, there a broken phrase;
Till, mastering large proportions of his thought,
I get the hidden cipher to his ways,
I learn his final, topmost price—
And in a trice
The victim's bought!

GEORGE.

How is it with me? I seem possessed with a strange and passionate desire to know the truth of those old days of Clarewell Friary. Very unlike our times, certainly, and· its whole spirit:—were they better, or worse? And I? Am I an usurper in the place of more faithful stewards?—who shall inspire me, to know? who shall solve that for me?

ANGEL.

They who their lives in straitness wore away
Trode here the narrower paths to endless day;
High o'er man's common standard rais'd their aim,
To loftiest perfection toil'd, and came!
If not—their doom be measur'd by their call,
For God's own temple-height gives deeper fall.
Furthest remov'd, or nearest by the Throne,
Holier they were, or worse, than aught thou e'er
hast known!

GEORGE.

Well, I cannot define it: I could not prove it

reasonable, even to myself:—these are unwonted tears in my eyes! Yet, stay—no mere impulse—let me pause, let me weigh—

WALTER.

D'ye know, I've often thought—nay, 'tis certain—no one can help—

CLAUDE.

What he's inclined to: why, even so have I, now. The difference between Socrates, we'll say, and Alcibiades—somehow, I can't at the moment express it as I would—

DEMON.

  Just so!
  Beyond all other classes
Who do my work, and reap the harvest in,
    Are those philosophers—ho, ho!
      Who now begin
      To teach the masses
That what their dulman grandfathers called *sin*—
    Is just a disproportionate accretion
      Of noxious gases:—

CLAUDE.

Come, sirs—your glasses!

Demon.

The cause of murder, fraud, and pillage
   ('Tis ascertain'd quite well
As the long problem's true solution—
Whatever gossips down the village
Still prate of judgment, conscience, hell—)
   Is, phosphor in the pineal gland,
   Or other morbid brain-secretion;

Harry.

Glugluġluglug! clear as a bell!

Demon.

A matter simply of the constitution,
Which no man in his senses would withstand.

Gilbert.

Everything finds its own place and level, d'ye see, in this system of things. Some are fond of musing, like George: those we'll call the Dreamers, or the Seers. Others, like you and me, *glugluglug*—have no objection to enjoy themselves: that's a simple difference between one philosopher and another, I take it.

Claude.

Why, our grandmothers used to frighten us, all about horns and hoofs, and so forth, as nurses threaten children in the dark, to keep them quiet.

Now, for my part, I don't half believe those old stories.

     DEMON.

 Aye, aye—their antient foe,
With scathèd being, all a-glow
  To work their doom,
 Tempts no man—no!
 For how should non-existence,
Abstract and bodiless, find room
In this fair world, where physics can create
  By causes all material,
   Without assistance?
 Demons must be impersonal, if ætherial—

     CLAUDE.

Sing hey, sing ho! to the greenwood we'll go!

     DEMON.

   Ho, ho, ho, ho!

     WALTER.

What an echo from that wall!

     CLAUDE.

I didn't observe it, till now. But I've a kind of humming-top in my head: perhaps it was that.

     DEMON.

 Th' electric spark alone produces action :—

Gilbert.

I've seldom spent a day of greater satisfaction!

Demon.

So *me*, in their alembic of conjectures,
  They sublimate
Into a pure abstraction!
These are the men who set my subtlest traps;
  My best bow to their doctor's caps,
  And great success attend their lectures!

George.

Strange—most strange! but an impulse not to be withstood: I must kneel, perforce. Spirits of the dead, are ye around me now? are ye even near? hear, if hear you may—help me, if you can help!

Souls of Friars.

Look down on him, Lord! enlighten him!

Demon.

Gr-r-r-r-r-r!

George.

You have entered into reality, and that for ever: you see the truth unveiled! Gaze on it for me, too, in my darkness—gaze and reflect its light on me!

Souls.

Have pity, O Lord! on him, and on us! *Miserere!*

DEMON.

Gr-r-r-r-r-r! could I but tear out his heart!

ANGEL.

Demon, give place! for "*Who is like to God?*"
O heavenly hope! my charge is tending home
After these watchful four and twenty years!
Alleluia!

GEORGE.

I need to know—I only need to know! not with
a barren knowledge, but that I may *do!*

SOULS.

Send forth Thy light and Thy truth, that they may lead him, and bring him unto Thy holy hill, and into Thy tabernacles! *Miserere!*

DEMON.

Gr-r-r-r-r-r! will nothing snap his thread?

SOULS.

May he follow on to know Thee—*Miserere!*

DEMON.

Couldn't I topple a corbel down upon him?—
Gr-r-r-r-r-r!

GEORGE.

Teach me to do thy will, for Thou art my God!

DEMON.

A strong wind would almost do it, from that tottering wall!

SOULS.

May he go in to the altar of God, to God who shall give joy to his youth! *Miserere!*

DEMON.

Is there no serviceable adder among these loose stones?

ANGEL

Holy, suffering souls! our God reward your charity—your release draws near! *Alleluia!*

GILBERT.

Where's George, I say? I shall positively go and fetch him.

DEMON.

Would they could all be induced to come and take him away! Anything rather than this—*Gr-r-r-r-r-r!*

GEORGE.

Lord, if I only knew!—that which I know not, teach Thou me!

DEMON.

He's drawing off—I shall lose him! maledictions be heaped on him!

GEORGE.

This ruined place—was its antient life pleasing to Thee?—Could I but tell—how gladly would I rebuild, re-people it—

DEMON.

Confusion!

ANGEL.

Alleluia!
They shall build the places that have been waste
    from of old;
And shall raise up antient ruins:
And shall repair the desolate cities,
That were destroyed for generation and generation:—
Alleluia!

GEORGE.

Lord, what wouldst thou have me to do? what with myself? what with all that is mine?

ANGEL.

Aid him, Lord! by the bliss Thou hast confirmed to me! *Alleluia!*

DEMON.

Gr-r-r-r-r-r!

SOULS.

By the perseverance whereto Thou hast sealed us! *Miserere!*

DEMON.

Gr-r-r-r-r-r!

GEORGE.

Speak, Lord! for Thy servant heareth.

DEMON.

Confusion!

ANGEL.

Aid him, by my fruition of Thyself! *Alleluia!*

SOULS.

By our assured hopes of Thee! *Miserere!*

DEMON.

Gr-r-r-r-r-r!

ANGEL.

Dear suffering souls, your charity be multiplied to you! *Alleluia!*

GEORGE.

Lord, I believe! help Thou mine unbelief!

DEMON.

Despair! despair! despair!

SOULS.

Thanks for him, Lord! patience for us! *Miserere!*

GEORGE.

I give back to Thee, Lord, what I should never have held for a day!

ANGEL.

Alleluia! alleluia! alleluia!

GUARDIAN ANGEL OF A FRIAR'S SOUL (*descending*).

Veni de Libano, Sponsa: veni, coronaberis!

FREED SOUL (*ascending*).

In exitu Israel: Alleluia! alleluia!

DEMON.

Gr-r-r-r-r-r-r!

GUARDIAN ANGELS OF THE OTHER SOULS.

Alleluia! Kyrie eleison!

DEMON.

Gr-r-r-r-r-r!

SOULS, waiting.

De profundis! Miserere!

www.ingramcontent.com/pod-product-compliance
Lightning Source LLC
Chambersburg PA
CBHW020923230426
43666CB00008B/1549